THE SOCIAL CINEMA OF
JEAN RENOIR

CHRISTOPHER FAULKNER

THE SOCIAL CINEMA OF
JEAN RENOIR

PRINCETON UNIVERSITY PRESS

1986

For Debra

CONTENTS

The idea for this book dates from 1978-1979 when I set about writing a critical essay for my *Jean Renoir: A Guide to References and Resources*. Cataloguing and annotating all of the available literature in French and English by and about Renoir, I observed that virtually no one had discussed Renoir's political activity in France during the thirties, a huge oversight in accounts of his career as a film maker. The short critical essay that was the result of this observation argued that Renoir's conception of the role of the artist-intellectual and the function of art had changed fundamentally between the 1930s and the 1950s.

My conviction of the rightness of this observation was strengthened in the ensuing years by a review of the films and a reexamination of the Renoir literature old and new. The present book shows the vestiges of its origins in verbal echoes and occasional repetitions from that earlier essay. And yet, my argument in support of the difference between Renoir's career in the thirties and his career in the fifties is not now quite the same as it then was. I do not at present believe that orthodox authorship studies can present this difference in terms that would speak to film in its historical specificity. I would argue instead that it is precisely orthodox auteurism which has obscured Renoir's political activism and elided the differing ideological positions—with their related thematic and stylistic distinctions—behind his work of the thirties and of the fifties. A more supple, in fact social, notion of authorship is needed to describe the intersection of films and history. I now think that persistent, unspoken assumptions underlying studies of individual authorship have produced a massive repression of Renoir's political allegiances and of the immediate social intelligibility of the films he directed. What might once have been called a critical "oversight" is rather a consequence of the very premises of auteurism.

How this massive repression came about historically, and with what consequences for the treatment of Renoir (and of other film makers) since the Second World War is perhaps the subject for another study. My introduction does touch on the crisis for the production of meaning into which a wholesale subscription to auteurism plunges us. The remainder of this book looks at a dozen films, all of them directed by Renoir, and tries to situate their textual strategies somewhat outside the sphere of single and determinate authorship by seeing them as the product of historical forces.

I have debts of gratitude to those who advised or supported me in this endeavour: my colleagues, Peter Harcourt, George McKnight, Zuzana M. Pick, Mark Langer, and Patrick MacFadden, who know well my preoccupation with Renoir's work; many fine students who have tolerated my obsessions over the years; Claude Gauteur for his extraordinary generosity in keeping me abreast of matters *renoirien* in France; Dudley Andrew for an exceedingly perspicacious reading of the manuscript; Tony Lhotsky; Joanna Hitchcock and Marilyn Campbell at Princeton University Press, who answered my questions patiently. Mrs. Hitchcock advised me well and saw this book through the press. Research was supported by a Leave Fellowship in 1979-1980 from the Social Sciences and Humanities Research Council of Canada, along with a grant from the Faculty of Graduate Studies and Research, and occasional monies from N.E.S. Griffiths, Dean of Arts, Carleton University, Ottawa, Canada.

Ottawa, Canada
July 1984

NOTE

Throughout this book, translations from the French are my own unless otherwise indicated.

THE SOCIAL CINEMA OF
JEAN RENOIR

FOR ETHNOGRAPHY

*If directors and other artists cannot be wrenched from their
historical environments, aesthetics is reduced to a subordinate branch of ethnography.*

ANDREW SARRIS, 1962

Jean Renoir is one of the most internationally popular and widely
respected of film makers. At his death in 1979 at the age of
eighty-four he left behind him forty films directed over forty-
five years from 1924 to 1969. Certain individual films (like *La
Grande Illusion* and *La Règle du jeu*) stand out, but the whole
body of his work has been treated to great critical acclaim. In
an extraordinarily productive lifetime, Renoir also wrote four
novels, a couple of plays, an autobiography, a biography of his
famous father, the painter Pierre-Auguste Renoir, and a pro-
vocative collection of incidental writings. Renoir is one of the
handful of acknowledged masters of the world cinema.

Not surprisingly, a great deal has been written about Renoir's
career as a film maker. There have been important books in
French and English by Armand-Jean Cauliez, Pierre Leprohon,
François Poulle, André Bazin, Leo Braudy, Raymond Durgnat,
Claude Beylie, Alexander Sesonske, and Daniel Serceau, and even
books in Italian, Rumanian, and Russian, as well as collections
of source materials in German and Spanish. Most of the full-
length studies I have cited, as well as shorter pieces like that by
Peter Harcourt, take as axiomatic Renoir's assertion that a film
maker makes one film over and over all his life.[1] By discovering

[1] Rui Nogueira and François Truchaud, "Interview with Jean Renoir," *Sight and
Sound* 37, no. 2 (Spring 1968), p. 61: "I believe that many authors, and certainly myself,
tell one story all our lives, the same one, with different characters, different
surroundings."

3

(or imposing) some stylistic or thematic pattern across all of Renoir's works, critics have tended to insist that all form one indivisible "master" film, one organic whole.

For André Bazin, Renoir's wholeness is defined by his commitment to a realist film practice, which is seen to exemplify his moral authority on man's essential and permanent questions.[2] Others have found continuity in Renoir's evident preoccupation with certain themes: Leo Braudy explores the tension between nature and theatre; Peter Harcourt the themes of passion, friendship, and nature; Claude Beylie claims that Renoir has consistently asserted that art is superior to life. As often as not these patterns of stylistic or thematic unity are verified by an appeal to the recurrence of certain basic motifs: master and servant relationships, the presence of water (rivers, swamps, snow), Naturalist plots (Renoir's supposed literariness), Impressionist allusions (from his father), the frequency of poachers or laundresses, gourmandizing, the repetition of names, lines of dialogue, incidents, character types, shooting through doors and windows, "deep-focus" photography, and so on.

Such a perplexity of perceived motifs or correspondences (and there are more) producing so many different readings (and there are others) would certainly seem to argue for the richness and variety of Renoir's collected output as well as to justify a healthy pluralism among his critics. And I would dispute neither the richness nor the variety of the work. Beneath the pluralism in interpretation, however, there lies a fundamental sameness of method and attitude: in every instance the critic assumes the integral unity of Renoir's entire corpus. This assumption is, of

---

[2] It might be objected that André Bazin, Renoir's most sophisticated admirer, is not an auteurist and does not promote the view that Renoir's *oeuvre* forms a coherent whole. While Bazin did indeed warn against the excesses of auteurism, he upheld the idea of the continuity of Renoir's career and regarded changes as caused by superficial exigencies: "... for all its apparent contradictions, few bodies of cinematic work demonstrate such unity." See André Bazin, *Jean Renoir* (New York: Simon and Schuster, 1973), p. 144, for this statement and the following two pages for its strained rationalization.

course, an acknowledged premise of author-centred studies of the cinema:

> The auteur critic is obsessed with the wholeness of art and the artist. He looks at a film as a whole, a director as a whole. The parts, however entertaining individually, must cohere meaningfully.[3]

Along with the a priori assumption that the whole *must* be greater than the sum of its parts, auteurism also asserts the singular authority of the author (usually the director) as the univocal and determinate origin of the text and, as a corollary, the way a work of art expresses the unique personality of its creator. Such an expressive theory of art promotes the author as the site of meaning in an essential, prelinguistic sense by proceeding from the assumption of a unified individual consciousness to acceptance of the idealist fallacy that the film maker has some definitive personal identity that transcends time and place, which is to say, history, and that remains constant through forty or more years of film-making. Once the motifs or correspondences across a body of work have been determined and assembled their synthesis is alleged to signify the artist's "vision" or "world-view." To say, "Renoir," for example, is to mean the man and/or a designated body of work that contains or transmits humanist values.

I believe that this position must be challenged. In the first place, Renoir has had not one career in the cinema but two (or possibly more), and in the second place, his works cannot be aggregated to form one indivisible "master" film expressing a single "vision" or "world-view" without the severest critical and historical distortions. It has long been admitted that the ahistoricism of the auteurist approach is a fundamental weakness. But the point, finally, is not simply that the auteur critic *chooses*

---

[3] Andrew Sarris, "Towards a Theory of Film History," in *The American Cinema* (New York: E. P. Dutton, 1968), p. 30.

5

to ignore the pressures of history upon particular films or groups of films, or upon the material conditions of the film maker, but that he is oblivious to the ideological determinations of a practice that make it impossible for him to do otherwise.[4] Every critical practice is grounded in assumptions and presuppositions that will govern and delimit the production of meaning, whether the critic chooses to be aware of the matter or not. Certain avenues of inquiry can be explored only at the cost of not exploring others. But it still seems necessary to insist, against the claims of its practitioners, that there is nothing inherently "natural" about the critical pursuit of the wholeness of art and the artist. Auteurism has cultural-historical origins and has been sustained by specific forms of social organisation in post-Renaissance culture and society. "Unconscious" values out of Romantic aesthetics about the relationship of art to the artist, rather than to language, society, or the reader, along with a social history that approves the unified and inviolate consciousness of the free individual, have formed specific critical convictions. The auteurist

[4] Because I am saying that the practice of auteurism is ideologically determined and sustained, and because I will be using the concept in a specific sense throughout, at this point I had better make it clear what I mean by ideology. I do not mean a body of doctrine, a set of abstract ideas, or policy in support of a political party. What I do mean is defined in Althusser's neo-Marxism (see Althusser's essay "Ideology and Ideological State Apparatuses," in his *Lenin and Philosophy and Other Essays* [London: NLB, 1971]). Ideology acts to represent to people their relationship to the world, in and through material structures and material practices in society, that is, through systems of representation—discourses (like films), myths (in the Barthesian sense), etc. Therefore, ideology does not belong to some realm of pure consciousness and cannot in the first instance be a matter of abstract ideas or beliefs. It is Althusser's position that there is no such thing as "pure" consciousness or "pure" experience unmediated by social structures and social practices; ideology is necessarily a matter of the *lived* relationship between people and their world. In order to sustain the existing relations of production, in order to sustain society *as it is*, the function of a dominant ideology is to make the way things are seem natural, to make the historically determined seem universal, to prevail upon people to accept the common-sense view of things, to assert the rightness of the "obvious." Ideology is therefore profoundly "unconscious." Andrew Sarris's easy dismissal of contextual studies of authors and films as nothing more than "a subordinate branch of ethnography" is couched in a tone designed to appeal to the "common sense" of every reader.

6

obsession with the transhistorical wholeness of art and the artist is necessarily at the expense of a different view of the nature and function of works of art in society.

This book is not an "appreciation" of the master, nor is it an attempt to explain the work in terms of the creative sensibility of their putative author. It is a rereading of some of Renoir's best-known films for their immediate relation to historical and social developments. If, in Renoir's case, we question the holistic construction author/work as the principal task of criticism, we may find answers that may be more productive than those which result from common thematic or stylistic traits across forty films in support of an essentialist portrait of the author. We will be freed to reread particular films, to attend to differences between films, or entire groups of films, that may be more radical than the similarities they seem to share. I am not so much interested in who speaks these films as in what these films say and how and why they say it. There are many forces of production, both cinematic and extracinematic, that determine readings for texts. As Roland Barthes has demonstrated in *S/Z*, a text is comprised of a "weaving of voices." In Renoir's case, disregard of these production forces, of these "voices" woven through the films, has led to some unfortunate (not to say wilful) misreadings. Contextualizing the films will permit me to argue, for example, that Renoir's themes of the middle and late thirties in France are ideological positions. In fact, it seems to me that the films of the thirties respond directly to the historical conditions of the Popular Front period, that they articulate values in the culture and society of the time rather than some presumed Renoir world-view. When such an argument is advanced one can expect to discover contradictions within particular texts in relation to specific historical processes, or between groups of films nominally by the same film maker (as between Renoir's films of the thirties and fifties), and consequently within the heretofore transhistorical and unified consciousness of the film maker. Renoir's career in the cinema will be seen as something less than homogeneous and whole. The quest for a conceptual coherence and a stylistic uniformity that binds works together may seem a "natural"—meaning ideologically determined—critical inclination, but it may not be the most productive way of clarifying the problematic conjunction author/history/text.

With 1939 and *La Règle du jeu* Renoir's career in the cinema changes from one of specific political commitment to one of a philosophy of idealism, each career exemplifying a distinct view of the function of art and the difficult role of the artist-intellectual. While a number of Renoir's critics have acknowledged such a division (although not quite on these terms), only François Poulle, in his interrogative *Renoir 1938 ou Jean Renoir pour rien?* (1969), recognizes that *La Règle du jeu* is the ideological turning point in Renoir's cinematic activity (for others it is only the thematic or stylistic fulfilment).[5] Plagued by the questions we have not been able to answer—and will not be able to answer to our entire satisfaction until a great deal more primary research has been done—Poulle tries to deal with Renoir's abandonment of France and the French subject, his departure for Italy in 1939 and then for America in 1940, and finally his adoption of a new philosophy, by examining his compromise with the socialist Zola in his adaptation of *La Bête humaine* (1938). Poulle's context is still not large enough, for there are numerous extracinematic

---

[5] Majority opinion has it that Renoir's career went into a decline after 1939, largely on the grounds that the later work does not live up to the expectations created by the films of the thirties. When the career has been divided, therefore, it has been for evaluative purposes or for reasons of convenience. Richard Roud, for example, in his *Cinema: A Critical Dictionary* (London: Secker & Warburg, 1980), writes about the films up to 1939 because those are the ones he likes best, while Tom Milne writes about the films after that date presumably for the same reason. Each, however, finds correspondences between the films before and after this date and so conceives Renoir's career as a whole ultimately unified by the personality of the film maker. So far as I am aware, only William Gilcher in his 1979 University of Iowa doctoral dissertation, "Jean Renoir in America: A Critical Analysis of His Major Films from *Swamp Water* to *The River*," asserts unequivocally that there are two "great" periods in Renoir's work which are stylistically and thematically different. Although it is not his purpose to argue the assertion, it is on this basis that he proceeds to an analysis of some of Renoir's American films as belonging to a "transitional" phase.

factors to be entertained in such an inquiry, but he has at least encouraged us to press in the right direction. He acknowledges that the films of the thirties have to be examined in relation to their social determinants. With the exception of Daniel Serceau's recent *Jean Renoir, l'Insurgé*, Renoir's critics have studiously ignored such a suggestion.[6]

The questions remain. What were the prevailing circumstances of production and the historical conditions within which Renoir worked? What of Renoir's political and social commitments during the thirties that would give a sharper definition to the terms within which his films of that period should be examined? What of the film texts themselves? How do they, in their matter and their forms, mediate prevailing ideological positions? Why did Renoir leave France, despite his deep and sincere statements of commitment? How and why did he arrive at his second career? I do not propose to undertake categorical responses to these questions. But some suggestions will have to be made, some positions proposed, if we hope to add to our knowledge of the films directed by Renoir during this period. We will thereby add not only to our knowledge of this period, but to all of Renoir's life in films, because I think that the work of this first career, in all its facets, is decisive for the epistemological and ideological shift that takes place after 1939.

By his reticence concerning the intersection of cinema and politics in the thirties, Renoir himself has done nothing to expose any contradictions between his prewar and postwar work. Evidently his quasi-Hindu ideas, picked up during the filming of *The River* in India in 1949–1950, that is, his so-called philosophy of acceptance, his stated personal belief in the oneness of all

---

[6] Not to be overlooked is Elizabeth Grottle Strebel's work on the defining characteristics of a socially conscious French cinema during the Popular Front period in her 1974 Princeton University doctoral dissertation, "French Social Cinema of the Nineteen Thirties: A Cinematographic Expression of Popular Front Consciousness." Although Renoir's activity is not Strebel's primary concern, she has published some of this valuable research as "Renoir and the Popular Front" in *Sight and Sound* 49, no. 1 (Winter 1979/80), pp. 36-41, and a related article entitled "French Social Cinema and the Popular Front" in *Journal of Contemporary History* 12, no. 3 (July 1977), pp. 499-519.

9

creation, his confidence in the balance of nature, has done much to mask these contradictions and lead criticism astray. More actively, his autobiography, published in 1974, dedicated as it is to the New Wave, seems written to what Renoir's most passionate admirers want to hear. The focus of that book is the idealism inherent in the seeking of essential "truth" beneath superficial "appearances." Renoir, as befits his later views, places morality above politics:

> The separation of mankind into fascists and communists is quite meaningless. Fascism, like communism, believes in progress. . . . But in the last resort one has to take up one's own stand. If I were forced to do so, with my back to the wall, I would opt for communism because it seems to me that those who believe in it have a truer conception of human dignity.[7]

Renoir did make that choice in 1936, and out of a more positive and less idealist commitment than the above back-to-the-wall reply might indicate.

No small part of the difficulty in establishing the vicissitudes of Renoir's career in the cinema has been the inaccessibility of his writings, interviews, and the reviews of his films from the thirties, so that a full knowledge of his activities during the period has not been possible. I think that now, since the publication of *Ecrits 1926-1971* along with some other fugitive material (mostly collected by Claude Gauteur), it should be possible to produce a comparative account of prewar and postwar statements and attitudes in order to separate out some of the more glaring contradictions and to begin the task of reading the films in the context of specific social formations.[8]

In Chapter One I look at three films—*La Chienne* (1931),

---

[7] Jean Renoir, *My Life and My Films* (New York: Atheneum, 1974), p. 124.

[8] Claude Gauteur is the editor of *Ecrits 1926-1971* (Paris: Belfond, 1974). In addition he has edited *La Double Méprise* (Paris: Les Editeurs Français Réunis, 1980), an anthology of contemporary documents on the Renoir films between 1925 and 1939.

Boudu sauvé des eaux (1932), and *Toni* (1934)—that herald Renoir's nomination as the film maker of the French Left in the later years of the decade. These films are distinguished by their contemporary settings, the topicality of their subject matter and, stylistically, by an inclination towards a naturalism at odds with the dominant practice of the day. Precise definitions of character and environment in class terms realise narratives that centre around problems of class difference or class conflict. Sometimes bitterly, sometimes humourously, they suggest that one's personal and social experience have been historically produced. None of these three films, however, is informed by a partisan politics. Under pressure from current events, it is with *Le Crime de M. Lange* (1935) that Renoir's work actively takes up the causes of the French Left and that he himself becomes a polemicist on behalf of the Parti Communiste Français.

From this moment through to the end of the decade, Renoir's films were constituted in the ideology of the reformist politics of the Popular Front coalition. To this end, they attempted to make history by changing society. In their ideological role these films of the middle and late thirties, which I deal with in Chapter Two, offered imaginary or fictional solutions to contradictions in lived experience, such as that between the interests of the working class and the bourgeoisie, or that between the increased socialization of the means of production and the entrenchment of capital.

Ways of seeing the world become ways of knowing the world. An ideological perspective is also an epistemological perspective. It produces knowledge, even if the knowledge produced is limited by the incomplete solutions that ideology offers. The production of a certain ideological recognition of the world in the thirties was designed to enable the spectator-as-subject of these films to pursue the policies of the Popular Front without in the least being brought to question the "obviousness" of these policies.[9] Thus are social relations made intelligible in and by ide-

---

[9] The phrase "ideological recognition," or more specifically "the ideological recognition

ology.[10] For Renoir in the thirties, the future intelligibility of social relations was predicated on the transformation of society, and, as we shall see, both his films and his extracinematic activity were devoted to that end.

Inasmuch as an ideology is by definition a closed system, incontrovertible because it (silently) elides what it is defined against, incomplete because it delimits available interpretations of experience, ideology proscribes the knowledge it may produce of the world. An ideology will not (cannot) produce any knowledge that threatens its premises. An ideological proscription of knowledge may be exposed, however, either by theorizing its limitations through an analysis of its materialization in systems of representation like film, or by taking up a position within an ideology that produces a different interpretation of experience. The collapse of the Popular Front and its politics in 1938, along with the onset of the Second World War, led to Renoir's dis-

---

function" of ideology in its material representations comes from Althusser's *Lenin and Philosophy and Other Essays*, p. 161. For commentary on Althusser's ideas concerning the constitution of concrete individuals as subjects in ideology for these representations, I am indebted to Rosalind Coward and John Ellis, *Language and Materialism* (London: Routledge & Kegan Paul, 1977), pp. 61-78 especially. They also use the word "intelligible" to pin down the role of the subject for the realisation of meaning in social relations.

[10] I use the word "intelligible" because I mean that the relations of society and one's place within those relations must make *sense* if the totality is not to fall apart in contradiction. The "sense" that is made will be imaginary (rather than real), but then, no society can exist without ideology. Establishing one's identity (one's place) so that one can act effectively within the social totality in the interests of a productive system of social relations is what ideology is all about. To act effectively means to ensure the reproduction of the relations of production, without which, in some form or another, no society can continue. According to Althusser in his "Ideology and Ideological State Apparatuses," it is therefore the function of ideology to contribute to the reproduction of the relations of production. This function can only be secured by constituting concrete individuals as subjects for recognizable ideological positions so that the place they take up, their site of meaning within ideology, will be "obvious," beyond question, admitting of no contradictions that might expose their real relations to their conditions of existence. The exposure of contradiction could create insecurity about one's (ideological) identity and frustrate one's ability to act productively in the interests of the existing relations of production. Unintelligible social relations, then, threaten to become revolutionary social relations.

12

placement from the site of meaning, the site of intelligibility of his filmic texts of the middle and late thirties.

The immediate consequence of this displacement for Renoir was a crisis of thought, an ideological crisis, which produced *La Règle du jeu*, a work whose pessimism about the prospects for social change indicates that it is only defined *by* the politics of the Popular Front inasmuch as it is defined *against* the politics of the Popular Front. More so than any other of Renoir's films of the late thirties, *La Règle du jeu* will not be reduced to the ideology of a specific partisan politics. The secondary consequence of Renoir's displacement from this site of meaning and value was his emigration to the United States and the disappearance of the social context for his previous work. This removal evidently led to a confrontation with conflicting ideologies produced by a different culture and social formation, thereby exacerbating the crisis of thought produced in the historical and social conditions in France at the end of the thirties.

Following the expense of spirit in a waste for social change during the thirties in France, Renoir's sojourn in America between 1940 and 1949 was a period of reevaluation, a term of trial, dotted with critical failures and at least one near success. In Chapter Three I will look at an alleged failure (*This Land Is Mine*, 1943) and the one near success (*The Southerner*, 1945) during this transitional phase. I have no doubt that this period of reappraisal was absolutely necessary, for the betrayal of political aspirations and the advent of the Second World War had seemed to invalidate the authority and influence of the artist-intellectual in Renoir's films and the social efficacy of art. The problematic which will be seen to inform *This Land Is Mine* and account for its curious narrative dislocation and forced closure is this very crisis concerning the role of the artist and the function for art. After the crisis produced by *This Land Is Mine*, what Renoir called his rebirth in the United States—and what we may call a reconstitution of consciousness in a new ideological perspective—is in evidence in *The Southerner*. The highly cod-

ified generic determinations of this film produce an idealist interpretation of experience that conflicts with the socialist ideology
of the politics of the Popular Front period.

In Chapter Four I discuss those films of the fifties that verify
the ideological and philosophical shift anticipated by *The Southerner*. When compared with Renoir's work before the war, *The
River* (1951) must be seen as opposing one closed ideological
system to another. The knowledge that *The River* produces of
the world is incompatible with the knowledge produced by those
earlier works. The intelligible system of social relations that the
ideological recognition brought to this film would sustain is not
predicated on the transformation of society since it is not supported by a politics of change. In fact, it is not manifestly supported by politics at all.

Renoir's films now offer new imaginary or fictional solutions
to the contradictions of our lived experience. They create new
positions for the spectator-as-subject to act within the social
totality. One of these positions, consistent with a philosophy of
idealism, defines the role of art in society. The ideology in which
many of the later films are constituted is an ideology of aesthetics.
As I shall argue, in these films art resolves the contradictions of
our being-in-the-world by offering us a momentary glimpse of
ideal harmony. It is produced as a representation of our achieved
mediation with nature (i.e., our own natures). Art offers us the
individual and collective dream of our desire for social harmony
fulfilled. As films about entertainers and entertainments, *The
Golden Coach* (1953) and *French Cancan* (1955) particularly realise
this new function for art and a new role for the artist. Whereas
social relations were once made intelligible through an ideology
of politics, they are now to be made intelligible through an
ideology of aesthetics.

Given the ideological (and thematic) incompatibility of the
prewar and postwar films, we must, then, reject any critical
approach to Renoir's work that begins by insisting upon the
wholeness of art and the artist. There is no transhistorical Renoir

"vision" or "world-view," no essential Renoir personality that shall be the univocal source and measure of value for every text indiscriminately. Because we are dealing with determinate and conflicting ideological perspectives, I cannot establish the organic unity of an *oeuvre* nor can I verify a pattern of coherence across all of these films. Renoir's second "maturity" in the fifties, as I will call it, does not then imply a development but a difference.

In the chapters that follow I do not attempt to discuss ("make sense of") every film credited to Jean Renoir as a condition of the distinction of authorship. And in the twelve films I do examine, if certain structures and themes are ascribed to Renoir, sometimes for convenience, that is because I want to remind the reader that this private, material history acts with—interacts with—public history (social, cultural) to produce the work we know and admire. It is not a contradiction, after all, to see the individual as an "ensemble of social relations" or, to turn a phrase, to see the social as an ensemble of individual relations. I believe that language and language forms like cinema are social, and that individuals are constructed in language in society. The sources of meaning, therefore, must be grounded in history. I begin the task of restoring Renoir to history and history to Renoir.

In undertaking this task across three decades of Renoir's work (rather than somebody else's work), "horizontal" patterns of film style, subject matter, generic interest, character type, setting, plot situation, and intertextual reference emerge within each of the major phases of this activity that I have identified. Each film is a field, every group of films a network, through which has been woven those "voices" that produce a relation, however complicated, to parallel social and cultural conditions. Across thirty years and several distinct phases, these changing patterns represent the history of Renoir's—and no other film maker's—tensions with his medium and his times. The advantage of focussing on the work of one film maker in this way is that we can see how his personal and social history make him the site for a succession of interrelated tensions that produce a rich and varied corpus. This, about any film maker or any artist, is always a singular phenomenon, no matter how plural his work. To explore a relation through difference within the history of the same seems to me to offer the best of both worlds. I can only hope that the reader, too, finds this a valuable way of looking at one film maker's work.

Perhaps studying Renoir's cinematic activity in its various distinct phases, as this book endeavours to do, will lead to future work that looks at these films in a "vertical" relation with other films by other film makers from the same moments in time. For the present, however, by examining pockets of films—two, or three, or four films—pockets determined by historical and cinematic conditions and distinctions, I hope to note the epistemological shifts and ideological contradictions of a discontinuous and heterogeneous lifetime's activity in the cinema.

PROTEST AND PASSION:
LA CHIENNE, BOUDU SAUVE DES EAUX, TONI

> *When will the cinema go into the streets? To describe the simple life of the people, to render the atmosphere of its labouring humanity, is that not better than describing the murky, overheated dance halls, the unreal nobility, and the all too familiar scenes of night life?*
>
> MARCEL CARNÉ, 1930

La Chienne is a film about property; that is to say, it is a film that illustrates how the economic forces of society determine personal and social relations. It is an unusually topical work for the French film industry of 1931, quite different from the plethora of rude farces (like *On purge bébé*, which Renoir also directed in 1931) or romantic comedies (such as Renoir's *Chotard et Cie.* of 1933) that monopolised French screens during the period. *La Chienne* is Renoir's first major work. It marks his graduation from the apprentice works of the twenties, their avant-garde follies and their ambiguous social criticism, launching him towards the political concerns of the middle and late thirties.

Maurice Legrand (Michel Simon) is a henpecked petit-bourgeois employed as a cashier for a hosiery company. One night, returning alone from an office party, he comes across a prostitute, Lulu (Janie Marèze), lying in the street, beaten senseless by her pimp Dédé (Georges Flamant). Legrand escorts her home. To escape his domestic discomforts and the entrapment of his job, Legrand forms a naively romantic attachment with Lulu and sets her up in her own flat. He also furnishes it with his paintings, for Legrand is a Sunday painter of some talent. Dédé discovers this talent and sells Legrand's paintings to the Paris galleries as the work of one "Clara Wood" (as impersonated by Lulu). By chance, Legrand meets his wife's former husband (Godard, presumed dead), and seizing the opportunity Legrand tricks him into a reunion with the shrewish Adèle so that he might leave her for Lulu. When Legrand goes to Lulu he finds her in bed with Dédé and realizes that he has been duped. Disconsolate, he wanders away, returns, and murders Lulu. Dédé is wrongfully accused, tried, and executed. Legrand is free, and at the conclusion of the film is seen with Godard, both *clochards* on the street cadging money from passers-by.

One can certainly read *La Chienne* as a psychological study of the brutal reaction of a naive man to the unmasking of his romantic illusions. Legrand *is* naive and his reaction *is* brutal, but I want to argue that neither the naiveté nor the brutality are to be explained so much in psychological terms as in social ones. The temptation to impose an exclusively psychological reading on this sordid tale of loneliness, jealousy, murder, and injustice limits other possible readings, narrows the scope of the film, and above all obscures its historical importance. An emphasis on the psychology of character leads to Peter Harcourt's evaluation of both Legrand's painting and his passion for Lulu as "retreats into fantasy" from the frustrations of his petit-bourgeois works and days.[1] On this account, the painting and the romantic idealisation of Lulu are compensatory pleasures in a luckless existence. Both must seem colourfully apposite distractions for a man caught in Legrand's oppressive daily round of unimaginative office routine and loveless home life. If we are to read the film as a social study, however, we will have to come to terms with the social function of both Legrand's painting and his infatuation with Lulu. On that account, their very appositeness makes them more like traps than escapes, acutely predictable traps as we shall see, because they have been ideologically determined for Legrand in advance.

[1] Peter Harcourt, *Six European Directors* (Harmondsworth: Penguin Books, 1974), p. 81.

I do not believe that a psychological reading of the film adequately accounts for the violence of Legrand's reaction at Lulu's duplicity (it gets explained as pathology) or for his eventual fate as a *clochard* (it is seen as "too easy," as evidence of Renoir's "moral confusion"). But these consequences of his disillusionment are so dysfunctional, so extreme, as to suggest perhaps an excess in the text indicating what was *always* the true measure of Legrand's helplessness to effect real change. Escape was never more than a deceiving prospect. The temperature of Legrand's violence and the social direction of his fate can only be read by taking full measure of what his painting and Lulu represent.

They are—to borrow a phrase from Barthes that seems useful in this context—"the alibi of an absence."[2] Legrand's dream of setting up house with Lulu surrounded by his paintings is not an enrichment but a further impoverishment of his social existence. They indeed represent something that is absent from Legrand's life, but they are not in themselves that thing, only a restless alibi. As I hope to show, they do not at all offer a cure for his petit-bourgeois oppression but are the further *symptom* of his alienation. What I want to argue, then, is that both Legrand's painting and his Lulu *extend*, not mitigate, the embourgeoisification of his life. Whatever they may be to *him*, they cannot be seen as "retreats" exactly, nor escapes. Because neither is an active, witting revolt by a man who knows fully the world in which he lives, they actually enmesh him further in the contradictions of his petit-bourgeois world. Since they are the only release he knows or can envision, in that sense they appear to be private fantasies (he has no awareness of the value of his paintings, aesthetically or economically, nor can he grasp the fact that Lulu is a prostitute), but in that sense too they serve to further the mystification of his real social relations.

Through his painting Legrand seeks relief from his cold and nagging wife and from a stultifying office (in which we see him

---

[2] Roland Barthes, *Mythologies* (London: Paladin, 1972), p. 141.

literally imprisoned by his cashier's cage). Painting is but a pal-
liative for his frustrations, however, because Adèle complains
like a typical petite-bourgeoise of the wastefulness of this activity
and of the needless expense it incurs. So painting already represents a contrary satisfaction in this environment. Not finding
entire relief through his paintings at home, Lulu promises satisfaction outside the domestic environment altogether. Or rather,
she promises an *alternate domestic environment*, created by Legrand to fill a lack, but created as an idealised version of conjugal
domesticity. I think it of critical importance that we recognize
the social meaning and value of this environment. We are shown
Lulu's apartment brightly lit—in contrast to the drab and clut-
tered space of Legrand's lawful marriage—with new wallpaper,
fresh white coverlets on the bed, Lulu in a light peignoir, a
window open to the Parisian sky, plants on a ledge, and a bird
singing in its cage. And there is an important if brief scene in
which Lulu displays for a friend the marvel of the hot and cold
running water in her newly appointed bathroom. Surely the
social meaning of the space of Lulu's apartment, this space as
dreamed by Legrand, this mise-en-scène as a metaphor for his
idealised relationship with Lulu, is its ideological value as a
representation of bourgeois domesticity circa 1931. This space is
the myth, the ideal, the "naturalized" representation of his conjugal life. And that is why, in Barthes's phrase, it is only the
"alibi of an absence," because it is a futile stand-in for a genuine
radicalization of the conditions of his existence.

Why futile? All that the petite bourgeoisie can envision is a
normative definition of change, ideologically determined by the
pervasive myths of the bourgeois class. It is in the appalling
nature of his plight that idealisation is the best Legrand can do.
An opportune passage from Barthes's *Mythologies* explains the
predictability of this attempt at definition:

> ... the big wedding of the bourgeoisie, which originates in
> a class ritual (the display and consumption of wealth), can

bear no relation to the economic status of the lower middle-class: but through the press, the news, and literature, it slowly becomes *the very norm as dreamed*, though not actually lived, of the petit-bourgeois couple. The bourgeoisie is constantly absorbing into its ideology a whole section of humanity which does not have its basic status and cannot live up to it except in imagination, that is, at the cost of an immobilization and an impoverishment of consciousness.[3]

Legrand's is not a finer nature dealt a blow by an unappreciative world. He is a man who acts out of frustration with his life, but finds that the only available image of change is provided by the representations of bourgeois ideology. (At least until Legrand's violence, the film offers no other possibility.) So there is nothing "private" about Legrand's fantasy and the place he would take up within the dream he attempts to live with Lulu—his place as protector, dutiful provider, and romantic lover—has already been prepared for him by this naturalized myth of conjugal life. When I say that the place he would take up has been prepared for him, I mean that it is always already a condition of his consciousness within the lived ideology, a virtually inescapable condition of his being in this world. He is subjected to forces that not even Lulu and her unscrupulous Dédé could have devised.

Such is the authority of the "naturalness" of the bourgeois norm that Lulu herself desires to be a little bourgeoise—only with Dédé, not Legrand—consequently, the importance of the scene in which she proudly shows off her apartment to an admiring friend. This apartment, this private domestic space, is the space of action and identity in the bourgeois world. As Renoir's films of the thirties are so effective at establishing, one *is* the environment one occupies (the function of the Lestingois bookshop in *Boudu sauvé des eaux*, for example) in terms of one's social identity. Physical spaces are socially specific spaces. In *La*

<hr />

[3] Ibid., my emphasis.

Chienne the apartment is, appropriately, the site of both passion and violence when Legrand discovers that the identity he seeks is unattainable. That this ideally conceived bourgeois environment extends the function of Legrand's paintings is confirmed when he brings his canvases to decorate the flat. Before Legrand had met Lulu he had painted a picture of a well-dressed woman standing at an open window beside a birdcage with plants in the foreground, an image that is replicated in two or three shots of Lulu at her apartment window, as though we were to understand that Legrand is caught up in a double mystification through this representation of a representation. Lulu evidently animates the place that the painting previously held in Legrand's life as the projection of his dreams. Consciousness and its material representation live in complete symbiosis.

Painting and passion are activities that mask for him but expose for us the contradictions of Legrand's social condition. As we discover, those activities make him more, not less dependent on that condition. Contradiction is found between the bourgeois norm as dreamed and Legrand's real economic status, between what his imagination would furnish as opposed to his pocketbook. To support Lulu and maintain the space of bourgeois domesticity Legrand must steal from his wife and his place of work (until he is dismissed by his employer when the embezzlement is discovered). He can only stay with Lulu because Dédé discovers that the paintings are worth money. Unsuspectingly, Legrand is forced to *earn* his relationship with Lulu by continuing to paint so that Dédé can turn a profit. Legrand engineers his flight from his marriage by duping Godard with a cache of money his wife has apparently hidden away. And when the truth about Lulu's affections is finally revealed—Legrand discovers her in bed with Dédé—what is also exposed is the totality of Legrand's entrapment (which includes Lulu and his paintings, as well as his home and his office). What is exposed—to us, if not entirely to Legrand—is that his real social relations are a function of economic forces, since love (sex) is finally presented in commodity terms, to be granted or withheld on the basis of its exchange value. This is transparently the case during the final confrontation between Legrand and Lulu when she cruelly derides his lingering romantic illusions by matter-of-factly insisting that he finish a painting that she needs for Dédé:

> *Lulu*: Tell me then, you'll be able to finish it? Your painting!
> *Legrand*: What?
> *Lulu*: I need it![4]

We must remember that Legrand's infatuation is for a whore, and that he has fallen into the clutches of this whore and her pimp who are in the business of trafficking in affections. Lulu herself is treated as property by Dédé, to be disposed for his profit. The final appalling revelation is of the idealist deception of a bourgeois society: love (romantic or conjugal) cannot exist independent of economic factors.

Of themselves neither Legrand's infatuation with Lulu nor his painting transforms his social condition, but merely serves to enmesh him further in its contradictions. It is only by inadvertence, when Legrand is driven to murder, that they lead to change. On the personal level, Legrand kills Lulu because his feelings have been outraged. Stumbling upon the betrayal of his bourgeois dream triggers the excessive violence that completely uncensored frustration can produce. That the apartment, the physical space and representation of Legrand's ideologically determined aspirations, should be the site of this violence is an irony not to be overlooked. Killing Lulu, therefore, must also be read as a revolt against his embourgeoisification—never mind

---

[4] *L'Avant-Scène du Cinéma*, no. 162 (October 1975), p. 23: "*Lulu*: Dis donc, tu pourrais le finir, ton tableau! *Legrand:* Comment? *Lulu*: J'en ai besoin."

that the character Legrand cannot verbalize this—otherwise the appended epilogue, in which we meet Legrand after the passage of some years, having dropped out of his class to the level of the anarchic, propertyless *clochard*, seems unaccountable. Apparently—and this is important in view of Renoir's work of the middle thirties—this fate is the only radical alternative the film can conceive to living the "alibi of an absence." Legrand's alienation is now complete. He is left empty-handed and empty-headed, *déclassé*, a tramp. By the final scene of the film Legrand appears to have no recollection of his former life. Seeking a casual tip, he opens a car door for a man who has just purchased a painting from an art gallery. The painting, which he does not acknowledge in the least, is a Legrand self-portrait!

As simple-minded and as nonverbal as Legrand is about the causes of his fate, he could not have done other than he has done. He is the dupe of forces he does not understand. And these forces are not only oppressive, they not only act on him from without, they act on him from within as well. Repression is but the internalization of oppression. Legrand's circle of frustration is the all-too-familiar anxiety state produced by the sex/money nexus of bourgeois capitalism. (A state recounted in many films, of course, in Douglas Sirk's American melodramas, for example, and most familiarly perhaps in Hitchcock's *Psycho*.)

So the drama of *La Chienne* is social *and* psychological; but Renoir makes it clear that it is only psychological *because* it is social. Renoir forces this congruity upon us by the treatment of Lulu's murder, a crime of passion given social resonance. By crosscutting the final confrontation between Legrand and Lulu with the street musicians, Renoir creates a fairly obvious synecdoche whereby the environment in which the murder takes place is larger than Lulu's room—by implication it is the whole of French society. Furthermore, the romantic love song of the street singer represents precisely that mystification of social relations against which the murder can be seen as a revolt:

> If I sing beneath your window
> Like a courtly troubadour
> Be kind, Oh beautiful stranger
> For whom I have so often sung . . .[5]

Showing the street musicians and their courtly love song at the very moment of the murder—we never see the act itself—contrasts with the repressed sexual frustration vented through Legrand's violence. (Legrand kills Lulu appropriately in her bed.) The contradiction that the song of the street musicians would resolve is exposed by Legrand's violence, while Renoir's crosscutting creates the dramatic, emotional, and intellectual tension at the very heart of the film. (Had Renoir's simultaneous direct sound recording of both the performance of the street musicians, with surrounding noise, and the dialogue of Lulu and Legrand been preserved by the producer, the effect would have been even more dramatic and socially resonant.)[6] Although the presence of the street musicians is not extradiegetic, and does not break the linearity of the narrative, the effect is in some measure that of Brecht's *Verfremdungseffekt*. Were Renoir to depict the murder with graphic directness, sympathy for Legrand might be lost in the sensationalism of the act; diverting our attention to the street musicians and then tracking the camera up the side of the building to peer in at the window from outside, so that we might observe the consequences of Legrand's frustration, despectacularizes the act of murder itself and permits an ironic awareness of the tensions at work in the scene. To grasp the effectiveness of Renoir's treatment, only compare the very different handling of the murder in Fritz Lang's remake, *Scarlet Street* (1945). There the scene has nothing of the social resonance of *La Chienne*, and consequently the protagonist's

[5] Ibid., p. 23: "Si je chante sous ta fenêtre / Ainsi qu'un galant troubadour . . ./ Sois bonne, ô ma belle inconnu, / Pour qui j'ai si souvent chanté . . ."

[6] For a fuller explanation of Renoir's technical intentions, see Christopher Faulkner, *Jean Renoir: A Guide to References and Resources* (Boston: G. K. Hall, 1979), pp. 77-78.

naiveté is merely exasperating and pathetic. Renoir's treatment provides the specatator with a knowledge of which his protagonist is incapable. Legrand does not have political consciousness, but he is in unwitting revolt against bourgeois norms and bourgeois values. For all Legrand's mute outrage, this is murder most articulate, and only the first of a number of articulate murders in Renoir's films of the thirties. However, unlike the milieu created for Amédée Lange in the later *Le Crime de M. Lange* (1935) or for Pepel in *Les Bas-Fonds* (1936), there is no communal support for Legrand's solitary action inscribed in the text of *La Chienne* (he has only the "support" of his fellow *clochard*, Godard). But then Renoir has presented us with a drama in which the emphasis is on individual rather than collective action, and he has yet to receive the political influence or engage with the production forces that will encourage him to extend its possibilities.

By a nice irony, Dédé is executed for the murder he did not commit, and in that respect the law has been served but justice has not been done. I assume it is a comment on bourgeois institutions that Dédé is not executed for his brutal exploitation of Legrand (and Lulu), or for his catalytic role in the murder. His punishment does not fit his actual crime(s). Renoir's presentation of the trial makes it clear that Dédé is incriminated by the telltale Parisian argot of his class (contrasted with the middle-class, "neutral" French of the judge), by his arrogant manner, and by his past, rather than by actual proofs of his wrongdoing.[7] Someone must pay for Lulu's murder (society cannot be indicted; the law assesses the personal responsibility of the "free" individual), and Dédé seems a likelier candidate than most. The conflict in *La Chienne* between justice and the law appears again in *Toni* (1934), *Le Crime de M. Lange, Les*

---

[7] The point is made by Michel Marie in a very interesting article on Renoir's use of sound in *La Chienne* (voice, music, effects), according to the social class of the characters and the social milieu of the action: "The Poacher's Aged Mother: On Speech in *La Chienne* by Jean Renoir," *Yale French Studies*, no. 60 (1980), especially pp. 228-229.

Bas-Fonds, La Bête humaine (1938), and, in a different guise, in
La Règle du jeu (1939). The calculated importance of this conflict
to the film is evidenced by Pierre Schwab's recommendation
that the structure of the source material, Georges de la Fouchardière's novel, be altered.[8] In the book the revelation that
Legrand is Lulu's murderer is held back until after Dédé has
been executed. By enacting the murder three-quarters of the
way through the film, Renoir places the question of the brutal
relationship between justice and the law, crime and punishment,
squarely before the spectator throughout the last two reels. In
this way, I believe, we are encouraged to dwell on the social
rather than the moral implications of this conflict. As if to add
the grotesque to the cynical, Renoir intended to stage a scene
of Dédé's execution just prior to the film's epilogue. Preparations
were underway, with Renoir planning to situate the camera at
a distance and obscure somewhat the spectator's view of the
actual execution, when the censor intervened and rejected the
scene.[9] I would speculate that Renoir wanted to increase the
intended shock to the spectator that Dédé should be excessively
punished while Legrand is in a manner free. Very cleverly,
however, we have never been encouraged to have much sympathy for Dédé, while Renoir's crosscut treatment of the murder
has taken the edge off our sense of Legrand's criminality, first
by eliding the act itself, and then by contextualizing Legrand's
plight within an entire society. We are led to concentrate on the
social meaning of Legrand's free state as a *clochard* in the film's
epilogue. The more closely one looks at *La Chienne*, the more
impossible it becomes to argue that it is simply a psychological
and moral drama when its presentation of social alienation is so
powerful.

[8] *L'Avant-Scène du Cinéma*, p. 24, n. 15.

[9] Ibid., p. 30, n. 19. On another point of adaptation, the film's writers took virtually
intact from Fouchardière the monologue in which Henriot, the hosier, dismisses Legrand, its conventional morality made to look sententious and ineffectual in the context
of the film.

We cannot say that the subject of *La Chienne* is explicitly political, however. Yet, the formal characteristics of the work, its narrative structure in particular, do serve to radicalize its substance. The prologue with the puppet theatre, for example, has Guignol disclaiming that what is to follow is either comedy or drama, the two conventional categories of the *boulevard du crime*. Rather than punishing vice or pretending to a moralistic attitude, the film will present characters who are neither heroic nor villainous, but poor types like ourselves. In other words, *La Chienne* will not be the usual bourgeois melodrama. If the film is "pessimistic," it is so in the sense that there are no heroes or villains; all are victims, or, more generously, products of an environment that they are unable to rise above or transform. Not Legrand, nor Lulu, nor Dédé (nor his judges for that matter) has any consciousness of the social and economic forces that have acted to strike them down. And if we arrive at the recognition that they are victims, I fail to see how that encourages us to accept our own victimization.[10] It is possible to act on the knowledge revealed. *La Chienne* simply refuses to be didactic. Perhaps this is the historical importance of *La Chienne* for us today: it refuses a facile and comforting closure to the contradictions it exposes. If we fully understand the social implications of the issues it raises we will have to think them through our own experience. Its topicality is our topicality. I take the dark humour of the film's epilogue, when Godard says that "it takes all kinds to make a world," after Legrand has told him that he has murdered, to be *our* privileged reaction to a tale of considerable moral and social ferocity, the film's final, cynical appraisal of the world it has represented. If we are disconcerted at being left with this difficult ending, so much the better: Godard's remark does not constitute the film's "moral," after all—that possibility

---

[10] This potential for acquiescence in one's sense of victimization is clearly what troubles Peter Harcourt about *La Chienne*. He reads the film as a kind of morality play about the impossibility of decision-making in a brutal world, and so concludes that it endorses a "totally pessimistic fatalism": *Six European Directors*, esp. p. 82.

has been rejected in advance by the prologue—and we are a long way from Renoir's philosophy of acceptance.

If there are further doubts about the authority of the film's ending, one need only consider *Scarlet Street* again. There guilt and responsibility are apportioned according to the ethics of bourgeois society, since the pimp is executed and the protagonist is condemned to a lifetime of madness, forever confessing his guilt out of conscience, yet never to be believed. Legrand never pays for his crime, because the social interests of *La Chienne* forbid an exact and reassuring correspondence between personal guilt and personal responsibility. The entire thrust of *Scarlet Street*, however, is individual and moral, not social, so that Lang's film *is* the usual bourgeois melodrama in which potential contradiction is resolved rather than exposed.

Renoir's prologue and epilogue place us outside his fiction, at least in the sense that they encourage our reflection, the former by its instruction and the latter by its tone. *La Chienne* challenges the prevailing ideological interests of bourgeois norms because it challenges—although it does not exactly subvert—the narrative codes at work in the discourse of dominant cinema (the unspecified temporal ellipses between sequences; the mixture of genres and tones, so that the film is now farcical, cynical, or pathetic; the absence of a neat and optimistic resolution that would permit the audience to leave the theatre secure and unthreatened). This is not a film that comfortingly reproduces the values of bourgeois life. The producer's consternation when he saw the finished film suggests that *La Chienne* threatened its economic function and was therefore a challenge to the ideologically acceptable (a situation that Renoir ran into throughout the thirties, and which doubtless accounts for the belated release of a number of his films in the United States). Only a mystifying publicity campaign, which tried to recuperate the film, momentarily tamed its threatening aspect and permitted its exhibition in France.[11]

---

[11] Renoir has frequently, and ingenuously, told the story of how his friend Léon

There are a couple of reasons why I have given particular attention to *La Chienne*. In the first place, it is a film seldom seen, at least until very recently, and about which very little has been written. But above all, its topical independence of the mainstream French film industry helps one understand why Renoir was recruited by the political Left in the middle thirties and why he was prepared to commit himself to its causes. None of Renoir's seven feature films prior to *La Chienne* manifests its bitter and direct criticism of the social formation. *La Chienne* is one of those films that, as Jean-Louis Comolli and Jean Narboni suggest in their "Cinema/Ideology/Criticism," refuses assimilation into the mainstream because it obstructs the clear passage of prevailing ideological positions. While not explicitly political, it nevertheless works "against the grain."[12] *Boudu sauvé des eaux* is another film that recognizes the practice of ideology and that attempts to interrogate dominant ideological positions as a means of deliberate action on social history. The success of its intervention is, however, another matter.

Boudu sauvé des eaux was shot in the summer of 1932. Adapted from a popular bourgeois comedy of manners and morals, its commercial success was almost a foregone conclusion. *Boudu sauvé des eaux* had had a long and profitable stage career before it went into production as a film. It was first performed at Lyon in 1919 with René Fauchois, the author of the play, in the part of Lestingois the middle-class bookseller, and in the next year it was taken to Paris. When it was performed again at the Théâtre Mathurins in 1925, Michel Simon played Boudu the

---

Siritzky—formerly of the Turkish navy, then a successful provincial distributor—agreed to show the film in Biarritz after Roger Richebé, the co-producer, refused to open it in Paris. As a means of attracting attention to the film, Siritzky devised a publicity notice which recommended that timid hearts had better stay away. The run was a success. Subsequently the film was brought to Paris and played at the Colisée. See Jean Renoir, *My Life and My Films* (New York: Atheneum, 1974), pp. 114-115.

[12] Jean-Louis Comolli and Jean Narboni, "Cinema/Ideology/Criticism," in *Movies and Methods*, ed. Bill Nichols (Berkeley and Los Angeles: University of California Press, 1976), pp. 22-30.

tramp. During 1931 and 1932 the play was revived and taken on tour.[13] Renoir chose an auspicious time to adapt the play to the screen, assuring himself of a commercial success. In addition to the reputation of the play and the standing of Michel Simon, who would play Boudu, the producers went a step further and hired Charles Granval, a celebrated stage actor, to play Lestingois.

After the uncertain reception accorded *La Chienne* by the industry, Renoir needed to regain his footing. But again, as he had done with his source for *La Chienne*, Renoir altered René Fauchois's play to suit his own ends. Like the earlier adaptation, these changes led to an exposure of bourgeois values rather than a defense of them. Radical liberties—not in a political sense, but in a dramatic one—were taken with Fauchois's play's construction, his delineation of character, and above all with the moral of his boulevard theatre piece. When Fauchois saw the results of the Renoir–Simon transposition he was greatly offended. For in the play Lestingois's bourgeois benevolence and progressive notions are to be taken seriously, and when he saves Boudu from drowning as a magnanimous humanitarian gesture he is rewarded by seeing Boudu tamed, educated, and civilised under his tutelage. Boudu becomes a converted loyalist to the ideals of the middle class, works in the bookshop, and remains to marry the maid in all good faith. So much for liberal culture in the first decades of the twentieth century. In Renoir's film, however, Michel Simon's portrait of the simple-minded Boudu seems like an extension of the unremorseful *clochard* with whom we are left at the conclusion of *La Chienne*. There, as here, his anarchism is instinctive rather than wholly deliberate. Boudu is irredeemable, a confirmed and not always subterranean threat to the fragile—and sometimes hypocritical—trappings of bourgeois respectability. He brings chaos into the bookshop and home: he

[13] For this information about the history of the play, see Claude Gauteur, "*Boudu sauvé des eaux* de Fauchois à Renoir," *Image et Son*, no. 184 (May 1965), pp. 49-56.

seduces Lestingois's wife (Marcelle Hainia); exposes Lestingois as a philanderer; will not marry the maid, Anne-Marie (Séverine Lerczinska); offends customers with his ignorance (he thinks a request for *Les Fleurs du mal* botanic rather than bibliographic); and spits in first editions (Balzac's *La Physiologie du mariage*). Fauchois was not happy with what had been done to his play, and to his morality, for over twenty years, until he saw the enthusiastic reception accorded the film at a screening in 1955.[14]

Why did Renoir so extensively alter Fauchois's play? The answer, rather obviously, is that he wished to promote the potential for class conflict that the dramatic situation offered. For Fauchois, bourgeois norms must have represented a more or less natural order of things to which the entire world might be expected to aspire. Boudu's metamorphosis in the play cannot point to any other conclusion. His difference is a momentary aberration that the guidance of a Lestingois can be expected to correct. In Fauchois there is, in effect, only one class (and not even a class really, but a universal human nature).[15] This is the self-righteous mandate of bourgeois liberalism.

It is not at all human nature with which Renoir is dealing in the film. The whole point of Renoir's revision is to preserve the sense of the incompatibility of two social classes and the irrevocable barriers between them. Renoir's interests in *Boudu sauvé des eaux* are avowedly social, not simply moral. To refuse to acknowledge this consequence of Renoir's substantive alteration of Fauchois's play is to dehistoricize the film and essentialize its characters. *Boudu sauvé des eaux* is not "a universal fable," nor is Boudu "a mythical being," a Los Angeles hippie "born thirty years too soon," or a model of Rousseau's natural man.[16] The

[14] See René Fauchois, "Réconciliation autour de *Boudu*," *Cinéma 56*, no. 7 (November 1955), pp. 71-72.

[15] This is the exnominating phenomenon of the bourgeoisie as explained by Barthes, *Mythologies*, pp. 138-139.

[16] Alexander Sesonske is the source of the phrases quoted, in his *Jean Renoir: The French Films, 1924-1939* (Cambridge: Harvard University Press, 1980), pp. 121, 139.

film is a comedy about class, as *La Chienne* was a drama about class. Boudu, and Lestingois, and Madame are as socially specific as are Legrand or Lulu or Dédé. These are the conditions for an examination of *Boudu sauvé des eaux*.

While I have invited comparisons in general intention with *La Chienne, Boudu sauvé des eaux* is the obverse of the earlier film; here Renoir puts on his comic face. If *La Chienne* is in a major key, *Boudu sauvé des eaux* is in a minor one. Perhaps the most telling comment on *Boudu sauvé des eaux* belongs to Raymond Durgnat: "If Lestingois had gone to the cinema to see *Boudu sauvé des eaux* he would undoubtedly have taken Boudu's side and laughed heartily at the 'other' Lestingois."[17] As Roger Richebé's anxiety indicated, one cannot say the same for responses to *La Chienne*. I interpret Durgnat's comment as an unintended judgement of the efficacy of *Boudu sauvé des eaux* as a work of social criticism. Let me stake out my position in general: bourgeois hypocrisies are indeed unmasked—conjugal fidelity, liberal humanitarianism, cultural guardianship—but unlike *La Chienne* no one has to pay a price for the unmasking. Two worlds collide, the untutored subproletarian Boudu and the educated middle-class Lestingois, and go their own irreconcilable ways at the end. The collision sparks humorous incongruities; the separation leaves matters much as they stood initially. The world has not really been upset, even if its processes have been questioned with a gentle satire.

Durgnat's remark supposes, quite correctly I think, that the ideal audience of *Boudu sauvé des eaux* is a bourgeois audience. No member of such an audience could fail to recognize himself in Lestingois and his milieu, so socially specific is the portrait. At the same time, no member of such an audience could take Boudu's "side" for the duration of the film and laugh at himself were he really the butt of a joke that actually threatened his

---

[17] Raymond Durgnat, *Jean Renoir* (Berkeley and Los Angeles: University of California Press, 1974), p. 88.

ideological position in the social formation. That this threat was never actual is supported by the enormously favourable press that the film received upon its release and by its great popularity.[18] The problem is that the satirical stakes in *Boudu sauvé des eaux* are never very high. Many of Boudu's grievances are against purely conventional bourgeois practices, in themselves superficial and trivial, even if they do sum up the foibles of a class. These include codes of dress (wearing a cravat, shining one's shoes, appearing coiffed and clean-shaven), proper etiquette at table (eating with a fork rather than one's fingers, using a napkin, acknowledging a good wine), and codes of general conduct (spitting in one's handkerchief rather than in books or on the floor, sleeping in a bed, treating one's benefactor with gratitude). The exposure of these foibles does spark much humour, as when Boudu demolishes the kitchen to find the kit for cleaning his boots and then overturns Madame's boudoir in a fruitless effort to get the blacking off his hands. It is outbursts like this that prompt Lestingois's belated reservation that one should rescue only members of one's own class.

Certainly we have no difficulty recognizing the absurdity of these wholly habitual practices of bourgeois life. The film also assaults bourgeois values at the audience's expense when Lestingois is forced to admit that they have a piano because they are respectable people or when Madame makes a great fuss about Boudu's wet bulk soiling her newly upholstered furniture after he has been pulled from the river. Mme. Lestingois's sense of property values is as strong as M. Lestingois's sense of cultural values. With both of them it is, of course, the appearance of propriety and respectability that counts. Lestingois's philandering is a tolerable veniality since it is equalized by Madame's submission to Boudu. The one trespass is humourously traded for the other in a discovery scene out of Restoration comedy as Boudu and Madame, in hot embrace, crash through a door

---

[18] See Gauteur, "*Boudu sauvé des eaux* de Fauchois à Renoir."

behind which is revealed Lestingois and Anne-Marie in each other's arms. That Lestingois's self-appointed humanitarian-ism—Boudu did not want to be rescued anyway!—is as hollow as conjugal fidelity is demonstrated by simultaneously announc-ing the seduction of Madame and the award of Lestingois's life-saving medal with a close-up of a wall print of a jolly bugler and the sound of a marching band. And finally, if Lestingois's bookshop represents the guardian values of Western culture—a bust of Voltaire, his favourite author, dominates the shop—their humanizing influence is effectively satirized by the hy-pocrisies that the characters actually live.

But I have already suggested that the stakes are not very high. The humour that is provoked at the expense of the Lestingois household and its class alliance is licensed by its inoculative powers. This is not humour that cuts, that subverts. To the contrary, a little laughter at one's own expense is a healthy thing. This attitude signifies a liberalism of which Lestingois himself would doubtless approve. Roland Barthes has described "the inoculation" as one of the rhetorical forms of bourgeois myth:

> I have already given examples of this very general figure, which consists in admitting the accidental evil of a class-bound institution the better to conceal its principal evil. One immunizes the contents of the collective imagination by means of a small inoculation of acknowledged evil; one thus protects it against the risk of a generalized subversion. This *liberal* treatment would not have been possible only a hundred years ago.[19]

If the humour in *Boudu sauvé des eaux* is inoculative, that is because it does not expose, attack, or question a "principal evil" of the bourgeoisie. To promote class conflict, to be truly sub-versive of the conventional privileges of the bourgeoisie, the film would have to make it clear that the ideological hegemony of

---

[19] Barthes, *Mythologies*, p. 150.

a Lestingois is sustained by economic interests. The film would have to point up the contradiction between, on the one hand, the myths that nominate this class and give it its good name in its own eyes—its humanitarianism, its conservation of cultural and intellectual tradition—and, on the other hand, its ownership of property and its exploitative social relations. I do not think such an expectation either extravagant or unjust, since the film raises the possibility itself both in the opening scenes, which I shall turn to in a moment, and in the device of the lottery ticket. It is not until Boudu is found to have won a hundred thousand francs, until he is in a position of property that is, that Anne-Marie is eager to marry him. At one ironic stroke of fortune, therefore, Boudu appears to have attained the final requisite to his complete bourgeoisification (at least in Anne-Marie's eyes), and at the same time to have conveniently exculpated the infidelities of M. and Mme. Lestingois. But just because the lottery ticket is primarily a device for facilitating the plot, the film does not seriously interrogate the real basis of the bourgeoisie's position of security.

The weakness of the film's social intervention can also be judged by its portrait of Boudu. For Lestingois, as for the middle-class spectator, Boudu is always and irremediably the Other: he is what they are not, and not likely to become (not so, incidentally, with the *clochard* of *La Chienne*), which again explains why one can safely take Boudu's "side" without threat and laugh "heartily" at Lestingois. Boudu's identity is strictly a negative term, a negative difference, against the positive term established by bourgeois norms. Such social specificity as Boudu has is entirely dependent on these norms. Boudu does not otherwise exist. Here, we might think, is insight of genius on the part of the film for its perception of the way in which the bourgeoisie appraises the world in order to preserve its idealist notion of an essential human nature. Except that for Boudu to have a positive identity, for him to be defined other than as an absence of bourgeois values, and for the film to pose a real threat to bourgeois authority, he would have to have political consciousness. That he does not have. As a revolutionary model, Boudu is as hopeless as Legrand. Perhaps Boudu's thoroughly negative difference explains why we cannot seriously believe that he will ever become a model bourgeois. Under Lestingois's tutelage he is too obviously a burlesque of bourgeois man—to the unending delight of the bourgeois spectator. His exaggerated coiffure, his ill-fitting suit (formerly Lestingois's) and absurd cravat, his show of smoking a cigarette, his lurching gait and his acrobatics (suspended in midair across a passageway, hanging from a door jamb, standing on his head), all serve to deride bourgeois man and yet diminish Boudu as a threat.

If Lestingois cannot transform the subproletarian Boudu into the very image of himself, reduce him to the sameness of his conformity, Boudu can only continue to exist as an exotic, a thing, a blinkered Caliban without the latter's poetry, which is the condition in which he began the film and the condition in which he ends it.[20] Therefore, to see him or think of him as a creature of (unspoilt) Nature—as some critics do—is still to offer him an existence based on an ideologically determined perception. And this is precisely how Lestingois first encounters him through his telescope as Boudu makes his way to the Pont des Arts to commit suicide: isolated in Lestingois's gaze from the real conditions of his existence, caught for the spectator by the iris on the screen, magnified under glass, Boudu is announced as "a perfect specimen." When he proves to be irreducible to bourgeois conformity, it is this state to which Boudu returns at film's end. With the otherness of the exotic we have reached the limits of consciousness of which this class is capable. So the social representation of Boudu is thoroughly reified; relation with him—for Lestingois and for the audience—is wholly and forever removed to the level of "thingness." This is why *Boudu sauvé*

---

[20] Another of Barthes's rhetorical forms in the grammar of bourgeois myth-making is "Identification," which is an account of the bourgeoisie's positions towards that which is Other to its own perceived nature: ibid., pp. 151-152.

des eaux stands as a film about class difference, not class conflict, a film of social criticism, not of social change.

Having reached this observation, I must insist again that *Boudu sauvé des eaux* is a comedy. What the dispelling laughter of this film serves to hide, the cynicism of *La Chienne* serves to reveal. Whereas the structural closure of *Boudu sauvé des eaux* as a formally "classic" comic text serves to put the spectator-as-subject ideologically back in place—the removal of Boudu allows Lestingois to reclaim both his wife and his mistress at the film's end, thereby restoring the spectator's security and assuring the full recuperation of the film as "innocuous" entertainment, so that potential contradiction is fully resolved—the structural openness created by the disconcerting tone of the epilogue of *La Chienne* serves to disrupt the expected confirmation of the position of the subject. Still, the conclusion of *Boudu sauvé des eaux* is more satisfactory than the sentimental dénouement of René Clair's *A nous la liberté* of the previous year. Renoir refuses to show Boudu and Lestingois at one with each other, nor, when Boudu dumps the wedding party into the river to plunge off on his own, does Renoir imply the facile solution that the way to freedom from bourgeois hypocrisy lies in the irresponsible world of the *clochard*. The very last image of the film is an extradiegetic, low-angle shot of a line of marching, singing beggers with the facade of a cathedral in the background, an internal montage that seems to signify the final irreconcilability of established values with the world of the *clochard*. Renoir, unlike Clair, no more recommends individualist actions as a solution in *Boudu sauvé des eaux* than he does in *La Chienne*. Do we count *Boudu sauvé des eaux* a success, then? Well, that really is to beg the terms of my discussion. Certainly it has been a critical favourite: Andrew Sarris has written a charming piece on the film.[21] It is known as an accessible film, popular with film courses, film clubs, and libraries.

[21] Andrew Sarris, "Boudu Saved from Drowning," *Cahiers du Cinema in English*, no. 9 (March 1967), p. 53.

Perhaps Renoir did fail to realize the potential for a more incisive intervention, a potential that is there in the film. I am thinking of the opening sequence with Boudu in the park after he has lost his dog. These scenes startle us more than the remainder of the film because they are *about* his "thingness," about the fact of his reification as a member of a particular class in society. Boudu lounges under a tree sharing a chunk of bread with his dog. A well-dressed matron gathers up her little boy and his toy sailboat and hurries away from this terrifying troglodyte. Perhaps she is shocked by the witty contradiction between Boudu's unkempt appearance and the fact that he is intermittently singing "Sur les bords de la Rivière," a popular song of 1932 which Renoir told Alexander Sesonske was about beautiful women and a freewheeling night life.[22] That song in these circumstances certainly confirms Boudu's alienation. When his dog disappears, he reports its loss to the park police, who brusquely tell him to move along. Boudu is not presumed to have any property rights. When an attractive *woman* reports the loss of her Pekingese to the same police and says it is valued at 10,000 francs, their response is immediate. The police respond to her because she has commodity value, both sexually and monetarily. Boudu is dismissed because he has none. Disconsolate, Boudu is next the object of sympathetic, if meaningless, charity when a passing mother and daughter offer him a five-franc note with which to buy bread. Wittily, and I suspect shockingly to the audience, Boudu then mocks the otherness of his social existence by handing the five francs to a man who does not have loose change to tip him for opening his car door ("What's that for?" "To buy bread."). In this rebellious act (I can think of no other comparable incident in the film), Boudu takes a step towards asserting a positive social identity by throwing the bourgeoisie's definition of him on its terms back in its face. This is borne out, I believe, by the total incomprehension with which the man

[22] Sesonske, *Jean Renoir*, p. 114.

responds to Boudu's gesture. In his continuing search for his dog, Boudu passes a poet (Jacques Becker) on a park bench babbling (albeit surrealistically) of romantic love. This encounter follows immediately upon the scene in which we see the woman who has lost the Pekingese being "picked up" by a passing motorist. The juxtaposition of these two scenes exposes another aspect of the contradiction of middle-class life, about as explicable to Boudu as its benevolent charity. The whole drift of this opening sequence testifies to an impassable gulf between Boudu and the middle class, while its comedy is less hearty and more bitter than the remainder of the film. The attacks on liberal-minded humanitarianism (philanthropy for five francs), on culture (the poet is mad), and on conjugal fidelity (the woman picked up) to be taken up later in the film are all here in brief, but there is no genial Lestingois to soften the blows, so that we can have a more detached view of the issues and may be conscious of a deliberate editorializing on the part of the film makers. Perhaps my sense of unfulfilled potential about these scenes also has to do with the authority of the visual style at work in the location exterior, an apparently casual style with direct sound that identifies a different mode of "the real" than that belonging to studio or theatre. When Boudu leaves the park and walks along the banks of the Seine towards the Pont des Arts where he will attempt suicide, the *prises de vues* of life passing on the street authenticate his condition in French urban society in 1932. At the bridge, too, where he jumps into the water, the camera lingers on the gathering crowd, includes the boats chugging on the river, and by keeping an extreme distance refuses to privilege Lestingois's rescue amidst the ambient life of Paris. It is not until the film enters the bookshop that we appreciate the specificity of the environment we have just left, the historicity of class contradiction and class conflict created by and in that environment. (Again, that is not the same thing as saying that Nature is somehow Boudu's milieu. The latter fancy is a bourgeois notion, as I have already indicated. And see Renoir's parody of classical myth in the film's prologue, consider Anne-Marie's song, "Les fleurs du jardin," as she dusts the artificial flowers on the piano, and so on. This is not a film about Nature opposed to nurture, but a film about class conflict.) Then, too, the potential for serious contradiction and conflict is further vitiated by the equal presence in the text of Lestingois and Boudu, perhaps a presence that is more than equal as I have suggested, since a middle-class audience will easily identify itself with Lestingois while protecting itself from the otherness of Boudu through self-purifying laughter.

Although *Boudu sauvé des eaux* may not represent an ultimate threat to any spectator's security, or to the structures of society, nevertheless there are a few important observations to be drawn from it. I would suggest that the setting in the park at the beginning and the care taken to represent Lestingois's milieu—despite my caveat above—indicate Renoir's awareness that social reality and character have been historically produced. And in so far as they have been produced by man, then they are part of a process that can be transformed (i.e., revolutionized) by man. The films of the later thirties will attempt open confirmation of this conviction. Did not Renoir insist, during this period, that environment takes precedence over the individual? ". . . man is shaped by the soil that nourishes him, by the living conditions that fashion his body and his mind, and by the countryside that parades before his eyes day in and day out."[23] And does not this prescription, as applied to *La Chienne* and *Boudu sauvé des eaux*, answer Marcel Carné's plea for a cinema of the streets, a contemporary cinema, a cinema without glamour?

In significant departure from his work of the twenties Renoir has chosen contemporary subjects, the everyday reality, together with a social concentration upon settings in which character and environment are a function of each other. The environment

---

[23] Jean Renoir, "Souvenirs," in *Jean Renoir* by André Bazin (New York: Simon and Schuster, 1973), p. 151.

from which the characters take their definition is a very specific environment, created by them, and creating them in turn. This is as true of Renoir's public places as his private ones during the thirties, his exterior settings as well as his interior. In so far as psychology of character matters to Renoir—and it has never mattered very much—it is rooted in place and specific historical conditions.[24] And the environment in which the action of Renoir's films takes place is the more specific, and contemporary, and socially concentrated, by his decided preference for a certain

---

[24] See Raymond Williams, "A Lecture on Realism," *Screen* 18, no. 1 (Spring 1977), pp. 61-74, whose ideas concerning the historical development of realism in the theatre have helped me: ". . . the room as the centre of the reality of human action: the private domestic room, which is of course entirely consonant with a particular reading of the place of human action—this is the life of the bourgeois family, where the important things occur in that kind of family room" (p. 66). Such is the importance of Lulu's apartment in *La Chienne*, as already noted, and the importance of Lestingois's bookshop in *Boudu sauvé des eaux*. On the other hand, this room is absent in *Toni*, precisely because *Toni* is not a story of the bourgeoisie. Perhaps, conversely, it is important for our understanding of *Partie de campagne* (1936) to recognize that we *do not* see the bourgeois family of this film in the security of its domestic rooms. In the country the family is out of its element. Consequently, it is vulnerable (compare the satirical implications of Monet's *Le Déjeuner sur l'herbe*). The country (the sweetness of the environment itself, Henri and Rodolphe) proves to be the family's undoing. Henriette can never be happy with Anatole after this excursion, and not because the country promises a better life than the one she knows, but because her affair with Henri has undermined the security of bourgeois existence and its values, which she took for granted and which she cannot escape. This explains the powerful emotional enigma of the look of contempt and loss she gives Henri at the film's end. I think that all of the film's energies are concentrated in this look, but I also think that one over-interprets the film if its social aspects are emphasised at the expense of its moving depiction of disillusionment as the price of sexual (and adult) awareness. Whatever one's emphasis, my point about the family's dislocation still stands. Perhaps it would have been more evident had Renoir filmed the two interiors of the Dufours's Parisian hardware store as he had intended. The dialogue for these interiors is reproduced in Pierre Leprohon's *Jean Renoir* (Paris: Editions Seghers, 1967). I believe, too, that the postsynchronized addition of Joseph Kosma's score and Germaine Montero's voice (at Pierre Braunberger's bidding for the film's 1946 release) further obscures the film's historical inscription and tends to essentialize its characters' feelings. This prominence given to the music track is most unfortunate since Renoir consistently downplays (and sometimes omits altogether) extradiegetic sound in his films of the thirties just because it tends to "universalize" actions, ideas, and feelings, and remove them from their socially specific determinations.

kind of realist practice (location shooting, direct sound, depth of field, long takes, camera movement). The force of this has always seemed more potent to viewers of *Toni* because action and performance have been so detheatricalized, but should be no less true for *La Chienne*, *La Nuit du carrefour* (1932), *Boudu sauvé des eaux*, and *Madame Bovary* (1934). *Chotard et Cie.*, a forgotten film, is excepted because its complete studio setting is so patently artificial, at the service of a narrative that has no more resonance than a situation comedy. It only remains for Renoir's development of an historical attitude towards society to be given political direction with his commitment to the Popular Front and his involvement with the Parti Communiste Français.

About the making of *Toni* Renoir has said:

> I saw *Toni* as the chance to really direct and to get free of the stupid conformism which afflicts so many of the people who run our industry. In short, *Toni* represented for me that liberty of esprit de corps without which no one is capable of doing good work.[25]

My sense of these remarks is that "the chance to really direct" meant the fulfilment of a number of tendencies that were developing from *La Chienne* through *Boudu sauvé des eaux*. Fortunately, a compliant producer, Pierre Gaut, gave Renoir carte blanche to proceed as he wished. As a consequence, *Toni* is the most antitheatrical, the most deglamourised of Renoir's films, and as a film about "labouring humanity" it is something closer to the bone than I suspect Carné ever envisioned or achieved. *Toni* is the first film by Renoir to be shot entirely on location with direct sound, for both its interiors and its exteriors, which in itself sets the film and the film maker apart from the mainstream of French commercial cinema in 1934. As the most naturalistic of Renoir's films, *Toni* picks up a thread in the history

[25] Renoir, "Souvenirs," p. 157.

of the cinema virtually lost since André Antoine's plea for a new naturalism as the proper responsibility of the cinematograph, and rarely discovered again until the advent of postwar Italian neorealism. The location work in *Toni* reinforces the topicality of the situation of Spanish and Italian immigrant workers in the south of France. Unlike *La Chienne* or *Boudu sauvé des eaux*, and Renoir's other four sound films thus far, there was no literary source for the story of *Toni*. The crime of passion that provided the idea for the film was drawn from life, a *fait divers* told to Renoir by a boyhood chum, Jacques Mortier, once commissioner of police at Martigues. At the same time, the depression that hit France with full force in 1932 and the resulting unemployment at the end of the year and on into 1933, especially among immigrant workers, must have enhanced the contemporaneity of the film's subject. The French government eventually went so far as to put an end to immigration and tried to repatriate foreign workers. All indications are that *Toni* was not to be a film of any time or any place; it was a film of that time and of that place.

Whereas until *Toni* Renoir had been involved in projects representing the middle class to itself (including *La Chienne* and *Boudu sauvé des eaux*), with this film he moved outside his own class for the first time to encompass a different social life to a (potentially) different audience. If Renoir was not to sacrifice the gain in naturalism and social relevance achieved by setting and subject, he would have to avoid "stupid conformism" in all aspects of the production. To this end, care was taken in selecting actors to play—without makeup—the physical and cultural types represented in the film. Most were cast in accordance with their actual social class and regional origin, and amateurs were employed for some of the secondary parts, such as the gendarmes from Martigues and the black worker. The majority of the professionals were from the Midi, and they were not discouraged from using the occasional dialect word or from speaking an accented French appropriate to their roles. For example, Charles

Blavette, who plays Toni, is a native of Provence, and speaks with that lilting regional accent, which adds an extra syllable to feminine nouns ending in "e." On the other hand, the foreman Albert is played by Max Dalban, a Parisian actor, and he accordingly speaks a northern French, suited to the social definition of his character. These linguistic (and cultural) distinctions prove to be essential to the conflict in the film. By designating the social specificity of his characters through their voices, Renoir rejects that stereotypical "speaking degree zero" (to adapt a phrase), the "neutral" French of the intellectual bourgeoisie that passed for the standard of realism on French screens.[26] As yet another bourgeois myth, the notion of *la clarté* prevailed in filmed dialogue as it did in literary discourse. To overturn it, as Renoir does here, and as he did in *La Chienne* and *Boudu sauvé des eaux*, is to recognize that its usage serves class interests.

All of the actors in *Toni* were relatively unknown. (Only Max Dalban had acted for Renoir before, in minor roles in six films.) While this circumstance might imperil the film's commercial success in 1934, for Renoir it meant not having to contend with well-known performers who relied upon proven and habitual effects, and it meant not having to conceive a film in terms of the established personality value of the actor. Fewer constraints upon the director would mean fewer constraints upon the actors with respect to verisimilitude in the interpretation of their roles. What Renoir wished to avoid was the artifices of representation that the French cinema traditionally borrowed from the theatre of the boulevards—the exaggerated gestures, the facial contortions, the overelaborate decors, the sentimentalities—despite the fact that his subject had all the ingredients of melodrama. In retrospect, *Toni* can be seen as the contrary of Renoir's previous effort, his adaptation of *Madame Bovary*, a film that now seems more than ever to have been a doomed excursion because of its

---

[26] Again, Michel Marie, in "The Poacher's Aged Mother," remarks upon this feature of Renoir's work and observes that there is rarely a character in the films of the thirties whose voice is not anchored socially.

unsatisfactory marriage of cinematic and theatrical codes. There, the deliberate employment of celebrated stage actors ensured that the style of performance and of speech would confound Renoir's brand of realist film practice.

What Renoir was after with *Toni* was a film whose story would develop before the spectator like an episode from daily life, in a style closer to that of documentary practice than to the codes of established fiction:

> Everything had been set to work so that our efforts would be as close as possible to the documentary. Our ambition was that the public would be able to imagine that an invisible camera had filmed the phases of a conflict without the human beings unconsciously drawn into this action being aware of it themselves. I was probably not the first to attempt a similar adventure, nor the last. Later, Italian neorealism would push the method to perfection.[27]

For all the inclination towards naturalism in the techniques of production, the camera is not the slave of nature nor does the camera see the world "as it is." There is no such thing as a reality "out there," which holds some revelation to the unclouded, innocent eye. Truth is manufactured by and through specific, historically determined representations of reality. I agree with Bazin that in spite of his apparent fidelity to external realism Renoir uses reality "as arbitrarily as Corneille used Roman history," and the film is rich and fascinating precisely because of "the contradictions which can exist between realism and truth."[28] I do not, however, agree with Bazin that this dialectic is "unintended"—for that is to ignore *Toni* in the context of specific realist practices in *La Chienne* and *Boudu sauvé des eaux*—and I do not agree that in consequence the truth here is "moral." With *Toni* Renoir's social observation—if we can call it that for

[27] Jean Renoir, "*Toni* et le classicisme," *Cahiers du Cinéma* 10, no. 60 (June 1956), p. 2.
[28] Bazin, *Jean Renoir*, p. 39.

the moment—serves the cause of social, not moral, realism, whereas for Bazin it is "only a means of experiencing and demonstrating the permanence of man and his questions."[29] That much idealism is a condition of Bazin's approval. The justification that Bazin finds for *Toni* makes his preference for the films after 1950 much easier, because there he recognizes a "moral evolution" towards a purer Renoir, "stripped of the dimension of social circumstances."[30] (The authority with which this evolutionary thesis is advanced manages to include the earlier films *and* obscure their historical specificity.)

Other critics have arrived at a similar conclusion. No one has failed to remark that *Toni* is a film in which feelings are extremely vivid and well observed. Individual passion, violent passion, has been regarded as the sole motive for character and the mainspring of the film's plot, so that the morality of the personal relationships is seen to be the essence of the matter while cultural and social factors are assumed to be circumstantial at best. Perhaps it is because Renoir has not explicitly analyzed prevailing economic conditions—there is not the slightest hint as to the historical causes behind the emigration of Toni and his mates in the first place—nor taken an evident political stand that there has either been a blind refusal to acknowledge the social meaning of *Toni* at all (Truffaut, Beylie), or else a tendency to privilege its ethical import over its social imperative by subsuming the latter under the colourful function of observation (Braudy, Durgnat, Harcourt, Sesonske).

But the notion of "observation" is too passive a justification for the unconventional naturalism of *Toni*. I want to depart from previous ways of looking at the film because I think that the passions or feelings of the characters arise out of a very specific cultural identity detailed by the mise-en-scène and the dialogue, and that the behaviour of these same characters is

[29] Ibid.
[30] Ibid., pp. 110, 145.

socially and culturally determined. In other words, so far as character is concerned, the causative factor in the narrative is not private (and singular) passion but a conflict within a specific social formation. In sum, it seems to me that the mode of "the real" insisted upon by the camera work and the setting for *Toni* authenticates the historical specificity of individual consciousness and cultural definition as created by and in the environment. It is precisely this practice that I want to examine by working outward from a sequence in the film.

The sequence is the first in the film to be located at the quarry where Toni and the other immigrant labourers are employed. It comprises three scenes and nine shots. The opening shot of two in the first scene establishes two figures in conversation at the entrance to the works, with trucks, pieces of equipment, and buildings behind them. All that we can note at this point is that we are dealing with an industrialized form of labour in which machines as well as men constitute the forces of production. Therefore we will likely be confronted with a work situation involving the division of labour. This is confirmed by what transpires in the next shot, a closer shot than the last, in which the two figures occupy a frontal position and dominate the frame. One of these figures is Albert, the foreman, dressed in a jacket and open-neck shirt, and this is our introduction to him; next to him is a company representative or government official, dressed in a suit and tie. One by one a number of labourers dressed in work shirts enter from screen left, have their papers examined by the official, and quickly exit. Albert passes the remark that national insurance payments are deducted from their wages. Both he and the official are French. All of the workmen are foreigners and all are unfamiliar to the viewer. They will not appear again in the film. They say nothing, except to acknowledge their nationality in a word. The shot belongs to Albert and the official because they are stationary and therefore dominant, clearly the masters of the situation, while the workmen are anonymous, virtually silent, glimpsed but fleetingly, and culturally different. This scene may seem inconsequential, but I believe it is important for the scene to follow and for the film as a whole because it establishes the basic social and cultural alienation of the immigrant worker. He has been forced to undertake wage labour in a foreign land out of economic necessity: "My country is wherever I can earn my bread," is almost the first line of dialogue in the film. The immigrant is *déraciné*, dispossessed; his expectation of happiness is brilliantly commented upon at the opening of the film with the shock-cut from the sound of the men singing of their hopes in the railway compartment as the open sea passes by the window to the dissonant shriek of the train as we see it thundering across the trestle from a low angle. "Do you think we'll be happy?" one of the newcomers asks on the road into town, only to be answered by a pan up to the empty web of steel and concrete over which the train has just passed. This, of course, is the same trestle that will figure in the film's conclusion, and we should remember it as the film's principal reference for an industrial way of life from which these people are also alienated. It is not, as critics of Renoir seem to think, merely a symbol of some universal fatality.

The condition of alienation established by the first scene of the quarry sequence is the keynote for the scene to follow in the quarry proper, and without it the dialogue between Toni and Fernand and Toni's argument with Albert would not make complete sense. The first shot of this series is the richest. It is a pan from the lip of the quarry at an angle down into the pit where we can see minute figures toiling with pick and shovel. As the camera pans it picks up Toni and Fernand at the quarry's edge and holds them in a high-angle medium two-shot while the background remains momentarily in focus. Needless to say, this is an exemplary shot from Renoir's work of the thirties, not simply because it satisfies Bazin's criterion of realistic spatial integrity, not only because it locates the characters in the physical environment, but because Toni's social condition is coextensive with the condition of other workers included by the shot and what he says and feels during the scene is determined by the space in which we see him. Moving the camera and shooting in depth does not so much emphasize the superficially transparent phenomenology of Renoir's screen image as the asymptote of reality—the latter phrase is Bazin's—as allow for the development of his narrative in space as well as through time. And in some measure that is the case here, so that one might say Renoir plays out his social narrative spatially while his narrative of individuals extends temporally, although it is, of course, the confluence of the two that actually constitutes the entire readable film. On the whole critics have preferred to discuss the temporal narrative, hence their emphasis upon passionate individual conflict to the neglect of social conflict. Eric Rhode, however, writing a film history, has found just the right phrase to describe the function and value for Renoir of the kind of shot I have been discussing: "his deep-focus shots, tracking camera, and multiple action within the image has the effect of socializing space."[31] Although Rhode does not elaborate, it seems to me that the socialization of space perfectly describes the dialectic that is effected by the mise-en-scène through camera placement and movement in Renoir's preferred settings. To put it another way, "the contradictions which can exist between realism and truth"—as noted by Bazin—are exposed in Renoir's work through the socialization of space. It is this achievement that distinguishes the murder scene in *La Chienne* and the opening sequence of *Boudu sauvé des eaux* with its specific analysis of class contradiction and class conflict in urban Paris 1932. By the socialization of space we should understand active social analysis rather than merely passive observation. With the formal and technical means at his disposal, Renoir undertakes social analysis in the quarry scene.

With men labouring in the pit of the quarry behind and

[31] Eric Rhode, *A History of the Cinema* (Harmondsworth: Penguin Books, 1978), p. 325.

below him in the image, Toni speaks to Fernand of his love for Josefa. He does not express his feelings in some abstract romantic outburst, but in a way arising from his social and cultural identity and his condition of alienation at this moment. Toni wants to make good wine! The desire may seem anomalous, given the physical space in which it is uttered—although I take that to be the point—but it is by no means silly. In the quarry Toni does not share in the means of production, must submit to the division of labour, and is cut off from his roots. By marrying Josefa he will be able to leave the quarry and work the farm with Sebastian, thereby realising the product of his own labour and achieving self-fulfilment. It must be made clear that Toni is not motivated by greed or property interest. Between the quarry and the farm Renoir is contrasting two kinds of work, two ways of life, two modes of being. Toni is a peasant, not an industrial worker, and if his feeling for Josefa is synonymous with making good wine that is because she represents the opportunity to reclaim his cultural identity.

The terms on which we are to regard Toni—as is usually the case with Renoir's characters—are not psychological, but social and cultural. The devaluation of psychology in the conception of character and character relations is one of the great attractions of Renoir's films of the thirties. The importance of this devaluation is as a recognition that the character as subject is not *self*-constituted, and therefore not comprised of an essential human nature, but is constituted in and by a plurality of discourses within any given social formation specified by the film. (In his writings Renoir has repeatedly put this in terms of man as a product of his environment.) As a consequence, the transformation of man and society always remains a possibility (asserted with more or less ardour, more or less directly, depending upon the ideological determinations at work to open or close the contradictions revealed by the film text: only compare, as extremes, *La Vie est à nous* and *La Grande Illusion*).

That Toni's feelings towards Josefa are sincere and his motives disinterested are confirmed with the appearance of Albert, whose behaviour and reactions are everywhere in conflict with Toni's because he is French, a northerner, and a foreman. By any criterion Albert is *un salaud*, and when he enters the shot after Toni's conversation with Fernand it is to exercise his authority as foreman and as self-perceived cultural and social superior by contesting Toni's right to dally with Josefa. Toni protests this supererogatory privilege by threatening to push Albert over the quarry's edge and telling him to stay out of "our" affairs and to stay away from "our" women. A succession of reverse-angle shots accentuates the tension that arises from sociocultural differences and linguistic confusion. When Toni speaks of "our" women he is thinking of their shared cultural identity—which perhaps helps explain why Toni loses interest in Marie, who is French—whereas Albert, with a very different cast of mind, can only grasp his meaning in property terms. It is as a sexual toy and for her exchange value that Albert desires Josefa. (In a characteristic expression he refers to her as "cette poupée-là.") Albert's greed, his ultimate contempt for work, and his degrading treatment of women have been quickly established.

After the confrontation between Toni and Albert, the sequence at the quarry ends with a setup similar to the first shot at the entrance and Albert roaring away on his motorcycle to accost Josefa. In taking Josefa by force Albert establishes his right of ownership and immediately sits down with Sebastian to divide up the real property, with Josefa considered part of the "livestock." Even while Albert is forcing himself upon Josefa, Toni, following custom, is suing for her hand with Sebastian through an intermediary, as though Renoir would suggest by the simultaneity of these events that Toni's way of life is hopelessly anachronistic in this alien land. Indeed, it should be understood that the tragedy that shapes the film and Toni's demise is not so much the tragedy of a hopeless romantic passion as the tragedy of an inevitable social and cultural conflict.[32]

---

[32] My use of the word tragedy is advised, not because I think the dimensions of *Toni*

While the form of labour in which Toni is engaged at the quarry is unquestionably alienating, and a material factor in precipitating the conflict in the film, it is not presumed to be the efficient cause of disaster. Renoir's ultimate concern, in the quarry sequence and elsewhere, is with those "unconscious" mental structures of a social and cultural nature that determine modes of behaviour and produce conflict.[33] In the film these codified forms of behaviour actually manifest themselves through speech, dress, food, kinship relations, and so on. I have already alluded to the differences that are signified by language and dress. Food is a source of marital conflict between Albert and Josefa, for when she serves him tomatoes and greens, a culturally familiar dish to her, he rejects it and longs for the steak and chips of his own experienced reality. Although this incident is but a detail, it helps to illuminate the basis for the dissension in the family that will provoke Josefa to shoot Albert. But it is the delicate matter of kinship obligations that puts most strain upon the Toni–Marie and Albert–Josefa relationships and leads directly to the climax of the film. Both Marie and Albert are uncomprehending when Sebastian asks Toni to stand as godfather to Josefa's baby. Not only is the de facto cultural significance of the request lost upon them, so is the de jure obligation that it entails. What Renoir manages to signify by this contract is that Toni's identity, his very emotional and intellectual being, is not with the French, not, specifically, with Marie, but with his immigrant kin. Because of the responsibility he has accepted Toni insists upon his duty of attending Sebastian's funeral. This produces his rift with Marie, her attempted suicide, their final separation, and Toni's long vigil outside Jo-

are Attic, as Claude Beylie evidently does, but because I think the condition that it poses, *as it poses it*, is unavoidable. Certainly we ordinarily think of tragedy as fate internalized—especially in its Elizabethan manifestations—and that is not the case here. Nevertheless, there is a feeling of the ineluctable consequences of a conflict that no word can better evoke and that troubles the social conscience. Tragedy it must be, but without making ordinary lives extraordinary for the sake of ennobling heroes.

[33] This facet of the film's concerns has been noted by Daniel Serceau, in his "1934: Un film précurseur, *Toni*, de Jean Renoir," *CinémAction*, no. 8 (Summer 1979), p. 68.

sefa's house until the night of the murder. I do not wish to assert that Toni's passion for Josefa is merely incidental, or that it is not in some measure naive—his dream of South America is sufficient illustration—but that this passion is not to be fully understood outside the determination of cultural factors and the alienated social condition of these immigrant peoples.

Albert proves to be no farmer, and under his management the farm falls into ruin and he into debt as he philanders with other women in the nearby city—evidently with women of his own nationality (the "blonde" at the cafe and the "skinny girl" at the post office are specifically mentioned). The irremediable tragedy of the film unfolds as Albert unwittingly destroys a way of life. Or rather, in view of the film's conclusion, I should say that through Albert, its unwitting instrument, one form of social life, one cultural group, destroys another. Toni's death has not been contrived by some inscrutable Fate of Attic proportions. It is played out in a context that urges an historical reading upon the viewer. In flight from the police, Toni dashes across the very trestle that carried him into town at the beginning of the film. As Renoir tracks with Toni his camera once again socializes the space of the action so that we may recognize the fatal contradiction between this web of concrete and steel, with the quarry works spread out in clear focus below, both symbols of an industrial age, and the run to freedom of a figure whose roots lie with a rural peasantry. (The contradiction is literalized through the contrast between Toni's ill-fitting, half-peasant costume and the technology that has contrived the physical setting.) Toni is shot down by Dominique, a propertyowner, the only bourgeois character in the film, and a secondary character for the most part, whom we see periodically protecting his daughters and his land by the same force of arms. It seems fitting that the only hint of class interests should coincide with the advancing forces of industry and technology at the moment of Toni's death. As Toni dies on the right of way another train arrives bringing a new load of immigrants. Renoir nearly repeats the film's opening

54

shots of disembarking labourers. Toni's individual drama belongs to a larger drama, which shall not so much be repeated
as extended until a particular social formation and its industrial
ambitions holds complete sway. Albert's murder was necessary
to free Josefa and Toni from personal and cultural oppression,
but the law of this land serves the interests of Albert and his
kind. The film does not lament, does not moralize over the
death of Toni; it reports; it witnesses an inevitable social and
cultural conflict.

In the three films that I have so far examined from the thirties
Renoir has satisfied Marcel Carné's plea for a cinema of the
streets and described the life of the people—the petite bourgeoisie and the criminal (*La Chienne*), the bourgeoisie and the sub-
proletariat (*Boudu sauvé des eaux*), the working class (*Toni*)—
described those lives as they had never before been described in
French cinema. In each of these films there is a rare *complot* of
individual passion and social criticism, illuminating the relationship between social being, conditions of work, and the private
passions of people. And the truth that Renoir analysed—interior
truth he has called it—was expressed by developing an unfash-
ionable tendency towards naturalism—exterior truth, so-
called—that produced a signifying practice at odds with the
dominant cinema of the day.[34] This signifying practice would
seem to have inclined Renoir towards historical modes of determining value, an inclination not necessarily at odds with his
own personal background of bourgeois liberalism.

And yet, taken together, it is difficult to deduce a common
intellectual attitude shared by these three films beyond the gen-
eralities mentioned above. It is difficult to deduce the intellectual
focus out of which they speak. Unquestionably, *La Chienne* exposes some specific contradictions of bourgeois capitalism, but
how deliberate is Renoir's analysis in view of the failed promise

[34] In later years Renoir quite frequently used this essentialist terminology to discuss
developments in his work from the twenties through the thirties. See *My Life and My
Films, passim*.

of the opening sequence of *Boudu sauvé des eaux?* And for all the gain in naturalism with *Toni*, strangely enough economic factors and class conflict per se seem to matter less here than in either *La Chienne* or *Boudu sauvé des eaux*. But perhaps this is unreasonable, even irrelevant criticism, for what I am admitting is the truism that a social cinema is not necessarily politically conscious. Without unwarranted prejudice to their achievement, not one of these films speaks out of a preconceived political position. Of course, in looking for a centre of (political) value I am anticipating, for with his very next film, *Le Crime de M. Lange* (shot during October–November 1935), Renoir does embrace a political framework to support his practice. Given his achievement to this point, one is not surprised that the French Left should have supported his work and sought out his allegiance. The affiliation now seems right and inevitable (although critics have been ignoring it for years).

One forgets, however, that when he embraced partisan politics Renoir effectively abandoned his experiments in naturalism. With *Le Crime de M. Lange* Renoir adopts a more stylized realism, the sort of stylized realism that will distinguish his work until the end of the decade and *La Règle du jeu*. At its most indulgent, with *La Bête humaine*, this style brings Renoir perilously near the atmospheric excesses and moralistic fatalism of so-called poetic realism as practised by Marcel Carné and Julien Duvivier. With *Le Crime de M. Lange* Renoir returns to the studio, and one consequence is a more calculated deployment of the camera—in this case he had the set constructed at Billancourt to the specifications of his camera movements—with less apparent carelessness in editing: in practice a less transparent camera style but a more transparent editing style. I think the obviousness of this practice is evident from the critical notice taken of certain privileged camera movements in the films after 1935, such as the 360-degree pan in *Le Crime de M. Lange*, the shot of Henriette on the swing in *Partie de campagne*, the opening shot of *Les Bas-Fonds*, or the shot that reveals the silent wonder of the soldiers when the costume crate is unpacked in *La Grande Illusion*, not to mention the plethora of attention-getting shots through doors and windows in all of the films of the middle and late thirties. When Renoir works on location during this period he applies the codes he has devised for the studio. This means that there is also a return to artificial lighting and noticeable makeup. There is a change, too, in Renoir's conception of character and performance. Rather than the naturalism achieved by casting actors of the same social and cultural positions as their roles, as he did with *Toni*, Renoir accepts actors who can create characters that represent the *idea* of a social type. This is as true of Jules Berry's Batala as it is of Pierre Fresnay's Captain de Boeldieu. This development has no better illustration than the casting of Jean Gabin as the working-class type in three films (*Les Bas-Fonds, La Grande Illusion, La Bête humaine*), a decision that exploits the established personality value of this actor from roles performed in other films of this period (Duvivier's *La Belle équipe* and *Pepe le Moko*, Carné's *Quai des brumes* and *Le Jour se lève*, Jean Grémillon's *Gueule d'amour* and *Remorque*). The cultivation of a more stylized realism in Renoir's work of the middle and late thirties is not necessarily a question of better or worse, but it did bring Renoir into the mainstream of French commercial cinema and into his period of public acclaim. As one appreciates, there were also political exigencies at work in Renoir's changing practice for the historic compromise advocated by the Popular Front.

TWO

AN IDEOLOGY OF POLITICS:
LE CRIME DE M. LANGE, LA VIE EST A NOUS,
LA GRANDE ILLUSION, LA REGLE DU JEU

> *Film directors are the sons of the bourgeoisie. They bring
> to this career the weaknesses of their decadent class. The
> public of the exclusive cinemas, who often decide the success
> of a film from the beginning, is also a bourgeois public. It
> is only after they have sanctioned a film that the cinemas
> of the poorer quarters hurry to pick it up. . . . Without
> delay, the cinema of France must be restored to the people
> of France.*

JEAN RENOIR, 1936

Renoir's contact with the French Left on *Le Crime de M. Lange*
(released January 1936) was effected by Jacques Prévert and the
October Group, a class-conscious proletarian theatre company
formed in 1932. Renoir could not have been unaware of the
political events of the year previous to the making of *Le Crime
de M. Lange.*[1] From the earliest days of 1934 various right-wing

---

[1] For a history of that most progressive theatre company, the October Group, see
Bernard Chardère's "Jacques Prévert et le Groupe Octobre," in *Premier Plan*, no. 14
(November 1960), pp. 71-91; and Madeleine Rebérioux, "Théâtre d'agitation: Le Groupe
'Octobre,' " *Le Mouvement Social*, no. 91 (April-June 1975), pp. 109-119. General histories
of the Popular Front period, in English, are not numerous. For much factual information
in this chapter I am indebted to Denis Brogan's *The Development of Modern France
(1870-1939)* (London: Hamish Hamilton, 1940); David Caute's *Communism and the
French Intellectuals (1914-1960)* (New York: Macmillan, 1964); and J. T. Marcus's *French
Socialism in the Crisis Years 1933-1936* (New York: Praeger, 1958). Especially useful for
its detail and for its inclusion of contemporary documents is Georges Lefranc's *Histoire
du Front Populaire (1934-1938)* (Paris: Payot, 1965). Information concerning French
cinema and the Popular Front can be found in Goffredo Fofi's "The Cinema of the
Popular Front in France (1934-1938)," *Screen* 13, no. 4 (Winter 1972/73), pp. 5-57. Further
details concerning Renoir's activities during the period may be found in my *Jean Renoir:
A Guide to References and Resources* (Boston: G. K. Hall, 1979).

organisations staged nightly demonstrations in the Paris streets protesting government corruption, principally the Stavisky affair. These demonstrations culminated in the riots of 6 February. On the 9th of the month the Communists and workers' groups responded with a counterdemonstration, which was brutally suppressed by the Paris police. An appeal for the unity of the working class against the rising strength of French fascism was published on 10 February by thirty-two prominent intellectuals, including Jean Vigo, Henri Jeanson, André Malraux, and Elie Faure. On 12 February began a general strike by Socialists and Communists, which established the desire of the two parties to make common cause against the threat to the stability of the Republic from the right wing. Through the remainder of 1934 and on into 1935, right-wing organisations like the Camelots du Roi, Francisme, Colonel de la Rocque's Croix de feu, and Coty's Solidarité Française remained conspicuous as governments came and went in efforts to find a political solution to the country's divisiveness.

To internal uneasiness was added external pressure with Germany's rearmament in violation of the Treaty of Versailles. On 2 May 1935, a Franco–Soviet accord was signed with the idea of containing Hitler by encirclement. The seventh Congress of the Communist International met between 26 July and 20 August in Moscow and formally adopted the policy of Popular Front alliances between the working class and the bourgeoisie throughout Western Europe to combat fascism. Sometime after 7 March 1935 (but before 27 July 1936), Renoir journeyed to Moscow to express solidarity with international Communism (an expedition undertaken by a great many fellow travellers during this period). On 14 July 1935, Bastille Day, the Communists, the Socialists, and the Radicals held celebrations in Paris to formalize their united front and to mobilize the working class against fascism at home and abroad. It was in this climate of perpetual crisis, therefore, with France in the midst of a cold civil war that was to last through until the autumn of 1938, that Renoir began to make *Le Crime de M. Lange*. His ability, his willingness, to respond to immediate historical events and the issues they raised had been proven with films like *La Chienne, Boudu sauvé des eaux*, and *Toni*.

Perhaps it is not irrelevant that *Le Crime de M. Lange* should have been made on the heels of the Stavisky affair. Although the film is well known, discussion of it has seldom appreciated fully the context out of which it came. Does the film not suggest that there is a judiciary to benefit those who have connections and can pull strings, or at the very least a system of justice that overlooks those who cannot manipulate capital and are at the mercy of clever (and dishonest) financial manoeuvres? However, I am not about to claim that *Le Crime de M. Lange* is in some manner an allusion to the Stavisky business or a political allegory of the times. It is simply a question of recognizing that, while government corruption is exposed during a period of weak economy, while the Parti Communiste Français is gaining support from the intellectual bourgeoisie, Renoir directs a film that idealizes the self-government of the working class. And whereas *Toni* had dealt with the social situation of unskilled peasant workers, *Le Crime de M. Lange* deals with urban industrial workers, a group more familiar to the film-going audience.

Unlike Renoir's subsequent films of this period with their more pronounced antifascist stand, the overwhelming emphasis in *Le Crime de M. Lange* is upon the boss, Batala (played by Jules Berry), the corrupt enemy of working-class consciousness and working-class solidarity. In the film we see something of Batala's entrepreneurial mismanagement: the overextension of credit has led to the abuses against the printshop workers and threatened them with unemployment. The conflict that precipitates the film's plot is not caused simply by the moral weakness of a particular individual. *Because* of his class position Batala is able to exploit others and behave destructively. The effect of Batala's exploitation is realized in personal as well as class terms, for the privileges of capital evidently include the coercion of women. Batala has seduced Valentine (Florelle), Estelle (Nadia

Sibirskaïa), and Edith (Sylvia Bataille). Without being in the least moralistic—in fact, the film is very funny (Jules Berry's stuttering, gestural performance not least of all), a kind of political swashbuckler with Amédée Lange (René Lefèvre), its naive, comic-book artist become a world-saver—Renoir makes it perfectly clear that Batala's abuses against women are consonant with his abuses of capital and labour. As the film indicates by Batala's abandonment of Estelle when she becomes pregnant and of Edith when he must flee his creditors, Batala treats women for their immediate use-value, just as he does the labour in his printshop and the capital he misappropriates.

The psychological as well as the social oppression produced by his actions can be appreciated in the scene where the billboard is removed from Charles's window after Batala has left. The scene is a choral moment in the film, since Renoir shoots it from inside Charles's room looking out into the courtyard where we may see the entire community assembled in celebration as the light breaks in. The symbolic, although completely unforced climax to the scene is the reunion between Charles (inside his room) and Estelle (outside the room) across the windowsill as she confesses her pregnancy and Charles accepts her nevertheless. Renoir's visual treatment encourages the intersection of the private and the public, the personal and the communal aspects of the scene, which justifies the subsequent claim that Estelle's baby belongs to the cooperative. The removal of the billboard and the reunion of Charles and Estelle is one of the community's greatest moments, since Batala has flown and everything he has represented (and done) has been erased. This moment of moral regeneration is followed immediately by the social regeneration of setting up the cooperative for the collective good. There is every indication that as the means of production have become socialized through the workers' appropriation of the printshop, so the form of the relations of production will be transformed as well. There is, however, one important reservation to this apparently favourable conclusion, and that is the presence of

Batala's principal creditor, young Meunier, the unassuming capitalist who holds the title to the forces of production but who
is willing to acquiesce to the cooperative ideal. How the film
deals with this contradiction I shall take up in a moment.

Unlike Renoir's films to that time, *Le Crime de M. Lange* is
thoroughly conscious of its politicization. Although its political
focus is usually attributed to the arrival of Jacques Prévert on
the production team, the original scenario devised by Renoir
and Jean Castanier is quite consistent with the thrust of the
finished film:

> It seemed to us that a crime of passion that is also a social
> protest, like M. Lange's, does not necessarily have to be
> situated in a sinister milieu. Rather, a study such as ours
> gains in dramatic intensity and in true humanity if it is
> surrounded by real everyday elements likely to amuse the
> public. . . .
>
> The film is based on the idea that any man who has
> carved out a place for himself in society and is worthy of
> his position has the right to keep his place and to defend
> it against one who would take it from him, even if the
> thief bases his action on legal principles.[2]

[2] "The First Version of *The Crime of M. Lange*," in *Jean Renoir* by André Bazin (New
York: Simon and Schuster, 1973), pp. 160-161. Incidentally, Renoir had a falling-out
with his longtime associate Jacques Becker over the direction of *Le Crime de M. Lange*.
The idea was initially Castanier's. He outlined it to Becker, who approached the producer
Des Fontaines with the proposition that he direct it as his first feature. Des Fontaines
lacked confidence in Becker's abilities after the experience of a very bad short film
Becker had made for him and he turned to Renoir instead. When Renoir agreed to
take the project on, Becker was understandably antagonized and retreated from his
friendship with Renoir for a few months. This *petit drame* is recounted by Castanier in
André-G. Brunelin's "Jacques Becker, ou la trace de l'homme," *Cinéma 60*, no. 48 (July
1960), p. 97. As Dudley Andrew has pointed out to me privately, the irony in all of this
is that the film itself is about exploitation (of labour, of ideas) for commercial profit.
Castanier, however, defended Renoir by insisting on the communal nature of film-
making with Renoir: "On the team which we formed with Renoir, no one had an idea
solely to himself. We worked with a community spirit. The essential thing was to make
a film that interested us, to make it together; it mattered little who signed it. And if
ever a film was the collective effort of a team it was that one."

So from the outset the film was conceived as a work of protest, and informed by a strong sense of social justice, with various comic elements evidently added to ensure audience popularity. While the vital contribution of Prévert is not to be undervalued, Renoir and Castanier were already responding to issues and conflicts at large in contemporary French society and were prepared to support the liberal political solution of increased socialization of the economy in the face of unprincipled capital interests. As for the precise extent of Renoir's personal awareness of political processes at this time in 1935, that is another (so far unanswerable) question altogether. Prévert was probably responsible for concentrating the action of the film in the courtyard and introducing the laundry (in the first scenario Valentine works for the publishing house), thereby emphasizing the sense of community. Much of the satire would also be due to Prévert through his association with the October Group, especially in the film's anticlericalism (Batala's disguise as a priest and his ironic cry for "un prêtre" after he has been shot), and in its representation of right-wing militarism and racism in the character of the concierge. But the visual concretization of the courtyard as the place of the film's action and the site of social change is accomplished wholly by Renoir through his systematic use of depth of field and a mobile camera to create the socialization of space in this microcosmic world. Renoir wanted the courtyard constructed in a studio (at Billancourt) so that the movements and setups planned for the camera could be executed to maximum effect. And in the outstanding instance of Lange's murder of Batala, the effect of the camera's extraordinary mobility is to politicize the tenor of the film beyond any doubt.

I have always felt that the film's political consciousness is confirmed more by the action of shooting Batala than by setting up the cooperative. Or rather, the political value of the latter initiative is only *earned* by the former action. When Batala was thought to have died in the train derailment, cooperation was made possible fortuitously. But the co-op can only survive *in the world* by eliminating the Batalas, and the film makers' decision to have Batala shot avoids the charge of an easy escapism in their promotion and defence of the cooperative ideal. Murder allows that a desperate solution is called for because of intolerable circumstances. As the young Meunier drives Lange and Valentine to the border where they will cross into exile a step ahead of the police, Batala's body is superimposed on the road so as to suggest that the way to freedom must be through his death. The prologue and epilogue at the border café (conceived by Renoir and Castanier in the original scenario) that frame the principal action are also essential to giving the film a purchase on historical reality, for they bring the conflict outside the microcosmic courtyard and locate it in the larger world. The device of the frame also emphasizes the centrality of the shooting over the setting up of the co-op, for Valentine's defence of Lange to a sort of jury made up of his working-class peers is intended to justify the former action, not the latter (or, again, the former in the name of the latter). And once again, by its framing device the film raises the issue of a social justice in conflict with the letter of the law, since it is on that distinction that the group at the café is asked to make its decision about whether to turn Lange over to the police or release him. Structurally, the prologue and epilogue have a function not unlike that which they serve in *La Chienne*. Locating the prologue and epilogue outside the principal action in place and time, removing any suspense by informing us of the murder at the outset, should encourage us to reflect upon the issues at hand as part of the makeshift jury. Presumably, we arrive at our particular judgement because we recognize our common cause with Lange against the unremitting selfishness of capital interests: "maybe he killed a rat," someone says. One can only conclude that the entire purpose of the film has been to execrate these interests and to idealize the possibilities of collective action. Surely no overt comment is required of the film makers to inform us that Valentine's story has raised the class consciousness of the group at the inn and shown it how it might act should the need arise. That is what the film is for.

Lange may be absolved by his peers, but legally he has not been cleared of Batala's murder (nor could he be). His uncertain future (the film's last shot is he and Valentine walking away from the camera across the sand to safety) is the price that must be paid for the collective freedom of the co-op. It may be, too, that this last shot represents an important mediation (or compromise, if one prefers) with the political realities of the day. *Le Crime de M. Lange* is not dealing with freedom in the abstract, either collectively or personally, but as it is produced by social conditions within and without the film. The necessary qualification that surrounds the very notion of freedom in exile as Lange's appropriate fate allows the film makers to defend the desirability of an historical transformation of society while stopping short of advocacy of militant revolution. Were Lange to stay and face the music for the murder of Batala, he would, after all, be condemned, while the *idea* of a cooperative as a model social enterprise would be considerably soured. Film censorship and the political expediency of the Popular Front coalition could not permit the consequences to be otherwise. Revolutionary initiative had to be tempered by the fact that this was a film—like all of Renoir's films of the period—made under a bourgeois democratic government.

There is no evidence that Renoir's position was ever that of a militant revolutionary. Quite the contrary. This brings up the presence in the film of the young Meunier, whom I mentioned as the reservation to the complete socialization of the means of production of the printshop. Unlike Batala, Meunier is a sympathetic capitalist, and he is there in the film because he represents the expectation that economic reforms might be achieved through the mutual good-will of the working class and the established bourgeoisie. As a character, Meunier is a buffoon (he has never heard of a co-op!) and so rendered innocuous, despite the vested private interests that he represents. We do not have to take him seriously, either in the dark little world of the cinema, or in the harsher, more demanding world outside. Between Batala and Meunier the film makers would have their cake and eat it. They would condemn the exploitation of capital and promote collective working-class enterprise, and yet accept the necessity of capital at the same time. This is a contradiction that the film cannot and does not resolve, and it was an insoluble dilemma for the successive Popular Front governments that came to power in France after 1936. The contradiction within the economic reforms proposed was between the increasing socialization of the means of production and the ultimate control of the forces of production by the owners of capital, a situation that materially affected the relations of production within the system. Governments feared that labour could not produce for need without the support of capital interests. *Le Crime de M. Lange* would *seem* to urge that we are well rid of the Batalas of this world, while representing young Meunier as "harmless." The film does end up qualifying its support for social change by admitting this contradiction, and for better or for worse it remains ideologically consistent with the reformist politics of the Popular Front compromise.

Again and again a murder is *the* decisive (central) act in Renoir's films of this period: *La Chienne, Toni, Le Crime de M. Lange, Les Bas-Fonds, La Grande Illusion, La Bête humaine,* and *La Règle du jeu.* And whether it is committed wittingly or not, the murder in all of these films can be considered a class action, and in most of them it is a crime of passion as well. Whereas in *La Chienne* and *Toni* the murders of Lulu and Albert respectively may be (narrowly) construed as psychological impulses, the shooting of Batala cannot be read in individualist terms. However, one cannot talk of the meaning produced by Batala's murder—or the murder in any of the films I have mentioned—without saying something about the *way* in which Renoir has shown it to us. And for critics of *Le Crime de M. Lange,* this has been one of the real conundrums of the film.

Why does Renoir's camera execute a 360-degree pan around the courtyard away from the direction of Lange's movement as he advances to murder Batala? The shot cannot be justified strictly in terms of the necessities of the plot. André Bazin has described, and diagrammed, the opposite movements of camera and character, and he has offered an interpretation:

> This stunning turn of the camera, apparently contrary to all logic, has perhaps psychological or dramatic justification (it gives an impression of dizziness, of madness, of suspense), but its real raison d'être is more germane to the conception of the film: it is the pure spatial expression of the entire mise-en-scène.[3]

Bazin is frankly not interested in what the shot may signify (it has "perhaps psychological or dramatic justification") as long as its manner of execution is consistent with the spatial conception of the circular courtyard set and the circular structure of the film. In other words, Bazin accounts for it in purely formalist terms. But this shot is not only the most "stunning," it is also the most bizarre shot in the entire film. The shortest distance between two points is not a 360-degree pan, and orthodox notions of continuity would (and did) find it hard to swallow, since its use had not been codified by established practice:

> The direction, with traces of genius, involves Renoir's usual disorderliness. Oh, those zigzagging pans. Blame it on lack of money. But also on a mania for improvisation, for "inspiration" on the set.[4]

For Peter Harcourt, on the other hand, this shot is accepted as "one of the great moments in the cinema," and he defends it on the grounds that it represents a typical moral uncertainty on

---

[3] Bazin, *Jean Renoir*, p. 46.

[4] Roger Leenhardt, "Le Cinéma: *Le Crime de M. Lange*," *Esprit* 4, no. 42 (1 March 1936), p. 977.

the part of Renoir's characters when faced with moments of decision:

> But the result of the way it is shot, in a double take from the courtyard with its vertiginous 360-degree pan that spins counter to Lange's movement, is again (one might argue) to blur the sense of the individual decision. . . . Lange, of course, does *decide* to kill Batala. But the way Renoir *stages* the scene gives us the sense that, like Legrand before him, Lange is not fully in control of his own actions.[5]

The problem raised by the shot is one of point of view. Why does Renoir's camera take us away from the central act in the entire film? The moral–psychological explanation seems to me as incomplete as Bazin's structural justification. If Renoir had wished to *insist* upon that attention he would very likely have given us the action from the murderer's point of view, working with shot–countershot as is customary, so that we might perceive it "as it actually happened," so to speak, thereby receiving the transparent force of a confirmed illusionist practice. I should think that the point is that Renoir blurs the sense of the individual decision by drawing attention to his signifying practice and detaching us from our passive consumption of the fiction. So the obligation, the obligation Harcourt feels, to judge purely *personal* guilt and *personal* responsibility must be relinquished. "Contrary to all logic" as this shot is, one does not get what one would expect according to the rules of classical narration.

The point from which the shot is taken (the centre of the courtyard) is known to the spectator, since we have seen the courtyard from other shots at other angles even though we have never had this setup before. Still, situating the camera at this point prepares for the complete desubjectivisation of the shot (if not the scene) in character terms when the camera suddenly

[5] Peter Harcourt, *Six European Directors* (Harmondsworth: Penguin Books, 1974), p. 85.

pans counterclockwise against the clockwise movement of Lange, thereby momentarily losing him to our view until he and the camera meet to shoot Batala. The issue is that the unconventional movement of the camera to the left, when we would expect a point-of-view shot along the 180-degree line of Lange's direction to the right, momentarily locates the "subject" of the film elsewhere than with the consciousness (or psychology) of the character. If subjectivity is relinquished, then where is the "subject" of the film to be found? If the camera (the film) does not enunciate the character of Lange at this moment, for whom or what does it speak? Clearly, the effect of this shot is to make our interpretation of Lange's character, of Lange's personal will and personal responsibility difficult if not impossible. What the camera (the film) speaks for at the moment of Batala's murder is that which is encompassed by all within view of the camera's circling movement, that is to say, the community. And because this shot is a formal breach of the text's predominant illusionist practice, it also enunciates the presence of the spectator as *object* and destination of the meaning of this active reading. Detachment from the fiction is the exemplary condition for one's own social practice. But for this extraordinary rupture, *Le Crime de M. Lange* proceeds on its linear way, adhering more or less to the grammar of classical narrative cinema, and allowing for psychological readings (although these still do not seem very productive). So the discontinuity of the shot, its displacement from the otherwise seamless linear narrative flow, depersonalizes it and should direct attention away from questions of moral–psychological value and towards a cognitive awareness that Lange's action encompasses a political will, the real political will of the entire community within the film and the potential will of the audience. Is Renoir's treatment here not a variation upon the Legrand murder in *La Chienne*, and with a similar purpose? If my reading is allowed, then one can see how it is consistent with the necessary qualification surrounding Lange's personal guilt and personal freedom at the film's conclusion.

In parenthesis, I do not think the reflective detachment induced by this shot is all that unusual in Renoir's work (it may be one of his recognizable authorial subcodes). Functionally speaking, there are other moments in other films by Renoir whose formal characteristics violate the transparent continuity of those realist surfaces so eagerly defended by Bazin. One thinks of the two examples cited, from this film and from *La Chienne*, or of the crosscut murder in *La Bête humaine*, or of the long shot of Octave conducting the imagined orchestra on the steps of the château in *La Règle du jeu*. I am not sure that Renoir's much celebrated practice of shooting through doors and windows does not occasionally function in this way; that is, interior framing with depth of field (Renoir's so-called theatrical compositions) can de-compose the transparency of space by calling attention to framing as an arbitrary code (much as an iris might in a contemporary sound film), thereby creating a presentational composition. An example that has the choric value one might expect from this practice, virtually with the weight of an editorial comment, is the shot from *La Grande Illusion* outside the window of the first barracks as the men gather in what seems a formal pose, drawn by the sound of fifes and marching boots. Each character comments on what the sound means to him as the camera tracks forward (*Boeldieu*: "J'ai une horreur des fifes"), until the equanimity of the diegesis is restored by a cut to a reverse angle. However, only a thorough analysis could establish the consistency of this practice.

Le Crime de M. Lange is a well-known film, but I have avoided enumerating those qualities that would continue to recommend it to the popular taste ("taste is merchandise," said Brecht). I mean to say that *Le Crime de M. Lange* has a social function that has been honoured rather more by appreciative gestures than critical analyses. Far from being the unique creation of Renoir's "personal moral universe," or confirming some monolithic Renoir "world-view," *Le Crime de M. Lange* is very much a product of specific historical circumstances. To plead that the film "transcends the politics of the moment" is to elect an idealist criticism designed to obscure the historical importance of the film for us today and mystify the political activism of the film makers involved.[6] Responsive to the political expediency of the Popular Front alliance, the film's makers have given *Le Crime de M. Lange* ideological currency by a number of clever cinematic shifts: acquiescence in the contradictory presence of young Meunier by treating him as a buffoon; the elimination of personal guilt in favour of collective responsibility in the murder of Batala on behalf of the community ideal of the socialization of the means of production as effected by the famous 360-degree pan; the class appeal intended by the prologue and epilogue, concluding with Lange's ambiguous freedom in exile, and a lingering question about the fate of the cooperative. Perhaps it was precisely the ideological function of the film—quite possibly passing unrecognized by the film makers themselves—that it should mask the impossibility of actually *living* any historical reality represented by such necessary hedges of qualification and contradiction. If film is one of the discourses by which we identify ourselves to ourselves, it may be that a film designed with the audience appeal of *Le Crime de M. Lange* can *only* represent the world as it is experienced through the prevailing ideology. We might say that *Le Crime de M. Lange* reproduces the mythified desiderata of the Popular Front. In three years' time, the parties to the Popular Front coalition would concede the impossibility of effective domestic or foreign policies under the political conditions they had created for themselves. *Le Crime de M. Lange* is but the first of a succession of films directed by Renoir through the remainder of the thirties to produce a representation of these policies.

Renoir's next film, *La Vie est à nous* (February–March 1936), represents an even more explicit political lesson for the times,

---

[6] Alexander Sesonske, *Jean Renoir: The French Films, 1924-1939* (Cambridge: Harvard University Press, 1980), p. 188.

produced as it was by the Parti Communiste Français for the electoral campaign of 1936. The campaign was, of course, Frontist, designed to support the alliance of the workers and the bourgeoisie against the power and wealth of the very rich and against the threat of fascism at home and abroad. The announced goals were frankly reformist. Renoir made his contribution in good faith. Given the compromises that sectarian politics was asked to make at this time, the Communist Party's revolutionary outlook may well have been "meagre," but it is a harsh judgement of *La Vie est à nous* to say that its program was that of a "benevolent protection society, an insurance company."[7] This judgement is harsh since it ignores the fact that the film was politically "correct," and evidently did the job it was intended to do. The Front won the April–May elections overwhelmingly. The issue of how radical a film—or any work of art—must be to be valid is always an historical one and can never be measured absolutely. Renoir's critics, however, have thought *La Vie est à nous* sufficiently radical to ignore it (Beylie), depoliticize it (Truffaut), or minimize its impact on contemporary history in a rather patronizing way:

> To be honest, though, it is mostly as a fetish or a totem that we render homage to this film today, for it is based on effects which are basically very naive. In fact, *La Vie est à nous* closely resembles a publicity film. Renoir resorted to certain didactic shortcuts which are rather simplistic . . .[8]

These remarks are representative. One feels that Renoir's critics have been embarrassed by the obvious and apparently uncharacteristic (for Renoir) didacticism of *La Vie est à nous*. Renoir's much vaunted humanistic sympathy and his impartiality towards all causes are contradicted by this film. But undoubtedly the real

[7] Fofi, "The Cinema of the Popular Front in France (1934-1938)," p. 23. Fofi is speaking from his own context of contemporary Italian militancy.

[8] Guy Hennebelle, "Jean Renoir (1894-1979) and the Militant Cinema," *Cineaste* 9, no. 4 (Fall 1979), p. 61.

cause of aggravation is the fact that this is a thoroughly tendentious film wholly financed by the Parti Communiste Français.
So critics have shunted the film off to one side, branding it
atypical of the director's work, an accident of circumstance, or
else they have disclaimed the significance of Renoir's contribution because he was but one of a half-a-dozen directors involved in its execution.[9] Since the form of *La Vie est à nous*
evades easy classification—fiction or documentary?—it has been
conveniently relegated to the status of a minor work. However,
if criticism were less concerned with assuming the importance
of the unified consciousness of the individual film maker or
asserting the organic wholeness of his *oeuvre*, and if Renoir's
lifelong work in the cinema were allowed more heterogeneity,
his political activity of the middle and late thirties would not
be seen as a mere nine-day's wonder but as a steadfast commitment. *La Vie est à nous* is but the most experimental manifestation of this among his other films, writings, and activities
of the period.

In *La Vie est à nous* the enemy of the Popular Front is represented as the two hundred wealthy families who strip France
of her resources for their private gain, thereby creating unemployment, dispossession, and social alienation. These two
hundred families were a real oligarchy of industrialists and fin-
anciers who effectively controlled the economy of France as the
largest shareholders in the Bank of France.[10] Urban unemployment resulted from France's perennial economic crises since the

---

[9] Jean-Paul Le Chanois, Jacques Becker, Jacques Brunius, André Zwobada, Henri
Cartier-Bresson, Pierre Unik, and Maurice Lime are all thought to have had a hand in
the direction of *La Vie est à nous* in addition to Renoir. For more on the production
history of the film see my *Jean Renoir: A Guide to References and Resources*, pp. 92-96.

[10] The justness of this criticism was borne out when the newly elected Popular Front
government under Léon Blum reformed the Bank of France and limited the power of
the two hundred families. The Blum government also dissolved the French fascist
leagues, including the Croix de feu. The account of the social and political situation in
1936 to which I am most indebted is Brogan's, in his *The Development of Modern France
(1870-1939)*, pp. 678-684 and 702-713 *passim*.

great depression. Peasant resentment against both government and landowners had been stirred by the falling markets in wine and wheat, while Pierre Laval's introduction of rent, wage, and price controls helped drive the disenchanted among the bourgeoisie into the arms of the Left. To the film's concern with domestic economic issues and their social consequences, one must add its concern with the fascist threat in the satires of Hitler and Colonel de la Rocque (the former is made to bark like a dog, while the latter is given to moving with exaggerated spasms). The threat of fascism had in fact grown since Hitler sent troops into the demilitarized Rhineland on 7 March 1936. No film more clearly articulated the platform of the Popular Front than *La Vie est à nous*, a platform put forward by Maurice Thorez on behalf of the PCF at the Eighth Party Congress at Villeurbanne in January 1936.

It does not seem to me that the social importance of *La Vie est à nous* is in the least affected by calling it a "publicity film"; that simply and accurately describes its function. A more progressive description, however, will entertain Brecht's advice that the politics of form is the form of politics. To this end *La Vie est à nous* institutes a signifying practice designed to intervene in the political transformation of French society in 1936. The innovation of this signifying practice involves more than the text itself, since it includes the independent financing outside the commercial industry through sums of money collected at party meetings, the unpaid services of its cast and crew (many of whom, like Renoir, were not Communists), a collective directorial responsibility (with Renoir the first among equals), distribution through Ciné-liberté (the film unit set up within the PCF's Maison de la Culture), and exhibition at union and party halls when it was refused a certificate of censorship by Laval's wary government. Among Renoir's works of the thirties, *La Vie est à nous* remains the only successful challenge to the prevailing conditions of film production, distribution, and exhibition. (*La Marseillaise* fell short of this goal, funding through public subscription eventually yielding to traditional methods of finance.) The producers of *La Vie est à nous* were aware that no film can wholly and successfully radicalize the politics of its form without radicalizing the form of its politics through changing (i.e., socializing) the forces and relations of its production. In view of the film's specific ideological function with regard to its audience at this particular historical moment, the signifying practices of its text are neither "simplistic" nor "naive" (Hennebelle's words).

The only thorough analysis of these practices has been undertaken by Pascal Bonitzer and his co-authors in *Cahiers du Cinéma* (regrettably unavailable in English), an excellent analysis that I will not repeat but only sketch.[11] The first sequence of the film with the children in the schoolroom demonstrates the complexity of the film's functioning. A combination (or rather, an alternation) of documentary and fictional passages permits the deconstruction of traditional narrative methods so that the film may unmask any pretense at transparency in the way it produces meaning and in the meaning it produces. Neither the documentary nor the fictional modes has an exclusive function; they are not mechanically opposed. They change roles and transform each other so that their interchange opens up gaps in the text for the intervening consciousness of the spectator, who actively contributes to the dialectical argument of a political discourse. In this way the film avoids the charge of a univocal didacticism such as occurs in *Triumph of the Will*, a film that so deliberately masks the way it produces meaning that one does not know whether it is documentary or fiction, truth or fantasy (oppositions that are, of course, conventional, not actual). Bonitzer and his co-authors argue that *La Vie est à nous* "thinks aloud" the process of its signification for the benefit of the spectator's active criticism.

It is worth examining how the relationship between picture

---

[11] Pascal Bonitzer et al., "*La Vie est à nous*, film militant," *Cahiers du Cinéma*, no. 218 (March 1970), pp. 44-51.

and sound and the alternation of documentary with fiction both change the status accorded each mode and produce a continual rewriting of the sense. The film begins with a succession of images of France's wealth (wheat fields, vineyards, the sea) accompanied by a "voice-of-God" narration whose authority is inseparable from the images as it cites supporting statistics. The style is that of classical documentary in which the matching of sound to image epiphanizes the "objective truth" of the images. A nonsituated medium shot of a speaker creates a shock of recognition that the voice-over belongs to a *particular* speaker commenting upon images that have not been produced by him. The narration and the images can now be separated and the "truth" of the latter localized. This conjunction produces the first gap in the text. There are more documentary images on the same subject followed by a long shot of the speaker in a schoolroom, which specifically identifies him as a teacher. He has not been addressing us, as we thought, but a fictional audience. The images can now be regarded as illustrations serving a special interest whose status as "truth" is relative rather than absolute. They are objective and not-objective at the same time since their documentary status has been transformed or demystified by a fictional context. Outside the school the children question the authority of both the images and their teacher by appealing to their own experience. We are invited to become aware that the "objective" status accorded the documentary images has been ideologically determined. They are a political fiction (the wealth of France is real, but not everyone shares in it equally) devised by the ruling class and passed on by the teacher. On the street we are presented with new images of miserable social conditions that match the children's questions. Here is a truer "document" (within a "fictional" context) of the historical moment, completing what was omitted by the opening images of France's wealth. In the form of a direct address to the audience on the model of Brecht, the sequence concludes with a workers' chorus—a different mode of discourse—summarizing the specific situation of crisis and intimating a practical solution: join the PCF, vote for the Popular Front.

This is how the first part of the film "thinks aloud" its process of signification. The first sequence is followed by an animated satire of the two hundred families; then a *Lehrstück* of the *haute bourgeoisie* at work and at play (target practice with standup cutouts of French workers); found footage of the riots and demonstrations of 6 and 9 February; shots of Mussolini, Colonel de la Rocque, the Croix de feu, and Hitler, contrasted with shots of Lenin, Stalin, men selling *L'Humanité*, and finally the office of its editor, Marcel Cachin. Cachin then introduces three successive fictional narratives dealing with social injustice as it affects urban industrial workers, a rural peasantry, and an unemployed bourgeois professional. These narratives are followed by rather lengthy political speeches by Maurice Thorez, Jacques Duclos, Paul Vaillant-Couturier, and others on behalf of the PCF as the practical solution to all of the documented and fictionalized problems that the film has presented.

The radical signifying practice of *La Vie est à nous* permits spectators a continuous interrogative relationship with the text so that they can analyze the conditions of their own social existence at this historical moment. By way of final reinforcement, the first images of the film are reintroduced at the film's conclusion, intercut with shots of a gathering crowd singing the "Internationale." The documentary "truth" of these images is in a sense reinscribed (France *is* wealthy) by conjoining them with shots of all of the actors who have appeared throughout the entire film. The actors are comrades and the images now belong to them, carrying the sense that these are the workers who have produced the wealth that is represented. The entire movement of the film—including episodes I have not discussed—justifies this final conjunction because it has shown the conditions that make it necessary to reclaim what belongs to the workers. What were once the images of ruling-class propaganda become working-class truth.

77

Because it has not seemed to fit in, *La Vie est à nous* is usually considered a negligible film in Renoir's career, whereas formally and stylistically it is probably his most extraordinary contribution to the cinema. My argument is that it has not been allowed to fit in, since its signifying practice makes it the most difficult of Renoir's films to recuperate for the dominant ideology of (pacific) bourgeois fiction, for the view of a humanist Renoir who transcends history and politics. The other films of the thirties can be universalized because they employ the forms of bourgeois fiction (despite all manner of subterfuge), although they, too, should be studied in a specific historical and political context. The politics of *La Vie est à nous* are essentially those of *Le Crime de M. Lange* and the films that followed it over the next few years.

Renoir's commitment is clear enough during this period, and when it was not being articulated through film it was expressed in a significant body of writing or related activities. Between 1936 and 1938 Renoir made six films, wrote some eighty-five articles for various journals, gave many interviews, and engaged in a number of ventures directly political in nature. *La Vie est à nous* was the only film Renoir made for the PCF (*La Marseillaise*, in 1937, was made for the Confédération Générale du Travail, the left-wing French trade union), but all of his extra-cinematic polemics were on behalf of the Party, in its publications or through its organisations. We should remember that the Popular Front government elected in 1936 was dominated by the Socialists and led by Léon Blum. Seventy-two Communist deputies were in the Chamber, along with 146 Socialists and 116 Radicals, but the PCF refused to take posts in the Cabinet alongside the Socialists.[12] Renoir stood with a party that was not actually in the government, but that still had to make the greatest compromises with its own political imperatives to lend its sup-

---

[12] For these figures I am indebted to Caute, *Communism and the French Intellectuals (1914-1960)*, p. 114.

port to the ideals of the Popular Front. This peculiar situation—endlessly repeated in Italian politics since the Second World War—permitted the Communists to criticize the government of the day as circumstances seemed to warrant. On the other hand, it permitted the government to reassure the doubtful among the bourgeoisie, and gradually to restore to capital some of the privileges it had lost during the reforms of 1936. Renoir, then, soon found himself in opposition to many of the government's official policy decisions, while in time, as we shall see, he would be open to disillusionment on two fronts. For the moment, however, as a known and energetic supporter of the Parti Communiste Français and a spokesman for the aspirations of the Popular Front, Renoir reached huge audiences in film and in print. Evidence of the contribution that his films made to the events of the day can be found in the critical debates that swirled up around each and every one of them, debates that more often drew the critics up along political rather than aesthetic lines.[13] In the light of Renoir's steadfast and energetic political activism, it now seems wilful to persist in saying, with Sesonske, that "Renoir's deep attachments have always been to people rather than ideologies; significant changes in his work have been influenced by particular persons or specific events rather than by adherence to a political party or program."[14]

Because Renoir's activities between 1936 and 1938 are all of a piece, it is possible to summarize them and draw some general conclusions.[15] Undoubtedly the most important venture with which Renoir was associated was Ciné-liberté, a PCF organisation that operated out of the Maison de la Culture as a branch of the Association des Ecrivains et Artistes Révolutionnaires.

[13] For the material of these debates see Claude Gauteur's splendid compilation, *Jean Renoir: La Double Méprise (1925-1939)* (Paris: Les Editeurs Français Réunis, 1980).

[14] Sesonske, *Jean Renoir*, p. 187.

[15] For some of the information concerning Renoir's activities and the function of Ciné-liberté I am indebted to Fofi, "The Cinema of the Popular Front in France (1934-1938)," and to Pascal Oury, "De Ciné-liberté à *La Marseillaise*," *Le Mouvement Social*, no. 91 (April-June 1975), pp. 153-175.

Ciné-liberté produced and distributed *La Vie est à nous* for the PCF (among other films). It came up with the idea for *La Marseillaise* as a film to commemorate the 150th anniversary of the French Revolution and acted as the organising committee behind the production. It also distributed *The Spanish Earth* in France (1937), with commentary and narration by Renoir. Ciné-liberté was launched as an independent production and distribution project, outside the confines of the established industry, and without the latter's profit motives: "Renoir was the focal point of the project, its leading light, and the mediator among the various points of view."[16] Its aim was to break monopolistic capitalism's stranglehold upon the industry—its financing, its choice of subject matter even—by bringing the people into film-making and by taking the cinema to them (hence, for example, the financing of *La Marseillaise* by public subscription and the voluntary services of thousands of CGT members among the cast and crew). Ciné-liberté also organised conferences on film-making and set up its own ciné-club with Renoir as president and Gaston Modot as secretary. At the peak of its activity the organisation reportedly had 20,000 members. To further close the gap between audiences and film workers, the magazine *Ciné-liberté* was published, with Renoir on the editorial board. For its first number, on 20 May 1936, he wrote a polemical defense of *Modern Times* in which he attacked the cupidities of French industrialists. Chaplin's film is also acknowledged with the closing shot of *Les Bas-Fonds*, an acknowledgement of the widening consciousness of the working-class movement. The importance of Renoir's involvement in the Ciné-liberté project must be judged by the challenge it offered to the existing forces of artistic production. In the context of other general reforms of the period, it sought to revolutionize those forces. It hoped to effect a change in the social relations between film maker and audience, and in the case of at least one film, *La Vie est à nous*, a radical mode

[16] Fofi, "The Cinema of the Popular Front in France (1934-1938)," p. 49.

of discourse was created as well. The government's censorship of that film is a tacit condemnation of its radical discourse and of the production relations that created it.

In other spheres, Renoir attacked the Popular Front Government's censorship policy, served on the editorial board of the PCF youth magazine *Les Cahiers de la Jeunesse* (to which he contributed seven articles), and gave his support to the Union des Théâtres Indépendantes de France. He urged the government to tax foreign films, dubbed films, and native producers who employed foreign personnel. When French producers, like others with investment capital, persisted in taking their money out of the country, he suggested that they were trying to sabotage the Popular Front. And he pressed French directors working abroad to return home and display their solidarity. In "Comment on fait un film" (written with Henri Jeanson) and in "Comment on découpe un film," both 1936, he attacked an exploitative production and distribution system that he recognized influenced both the forces and the forms of artistic production. In his most class-conscious piece, "Le Veau d'or photogénique," Renoir had the following to say:

> Film directors are the sons of the bourgeoisie. They bring to this career the weaknesses of their decadent class. The public of the exclusive cinemas, who often decide the success of a film from the beginning, is also a bourgeois public. It's only after they have sanctioned a film that the cinemas of the poorer quarters hurry to pick it up. ... Without delay, the cinema of France must be restored to the people of France.[17]

Elsewhere Renoir defended the introduction of a forty-hour week without loss in pay, collective bargaining, and other reforms in the conditions of employment in the film industry that

[17] Jean Renoir, *Ecrits 1926-1971*, ed. Claude Gauteur (Paris: Belfond, 1974), pp. 81-82.

had been brought about by the spontaneous labour stoppages across the nation between 7 June and 20 June 1936. Renoir, it would appear, was indefatigable.

One should also remember that during the summer of 1936 Renoir shot *Partie de campagne* (not released until 1946), an apparently anomalous work, since its primary theme—at least in the film as we have it—is not consistent with his political concerns of the period. *Partie de campagne* seems a beautiful anachronism, considering the turbulence of the times. While that judgement does not in the least affect one's pleasure in the achievement, one still wonders whether the film would have reflected the period more directly had Renoir had time to complete it. As it was, of course, no one excepting those involved in the production had the least inkling what the film was about. Renoir left *Partie de campagne* about 25 August to shoot *Les Bas-Fonds*, adapted by Charles Spaak from the Gorki play, through September and early October. Certainly this is a Frontist film, but unlike *Le Crime de M. Lange*, with which it bears comparison, it lacks authority. Here, too, the protagonist Pepel (Jean Gabin) commits a murder, which is handled by Renoir in such a way as to represent it as a class action on behalf of the community at the flophouse. But whereas the prologue and epilogue of the earlier film serve to create a social context for Lange's act in the larger world, no such context is available here. Furthermore, guilt and responsibility for the murder fall squarely upon Pepel, despite the filming of the murder scene so as to blur his individuality, since we are given a shot of him leaving prison after presumably having paid for his crime. Inasmuch as the law and justice are only nominally in conflict, what Pepel has done cannot really be construed as representing any threat to established interests. Pepel and Natasha (Junie Astor) leave the flophouse voluntarily—unlike Lange's and Valentine's leave-taking of the courtyard—although conditions there have not been ameliorated, nor is there any evidence of prospective social change. Pepel's and Natasha's dream of a better life has no foundation and it is neither deserved nor earned. The conclusion of *Les Bas-Fonds*, with Pepel and Natasha disappearing down the road, does not function in the same way to the same purpose as the conclusion of *Le Crime de M. Lange*. It is so much hollow idealism. *Les Bas-Fonds* should have given comfort to his reactionary enemies, but when it was released in December 1936 Renoir received the antiestablishment Prix Louis Delluc and the public congratulations of Jacques Duclos on behalf of the Parti Communiste Français, largely, one supposes, on the strength of the comment—rather than threat—that the film's company of outcasts made upon the social order. In addition, the Communists might have enjoyed the Frontist inspired interclass relationship between the Baron (Louis Jouvet) and Pepel, and their complicit disregard for the interests of private property, since one is an embezzler and the other a thief. But probably the award was made because, as the designated film maker of the Left, Renoir continued to soldier faithfully for the Party.

In November of 1936 he signed a public statement in support of the Soviet Union's foreign policy over Spain and over Abyssinia (Blum vacillated because of France's delicate relations with Mussolini). When Blum finally declared a noninterventionist stand towards Spain in January 1937, he created an irreparable breach between the government and the Left. The Loyalist Spanish government was also an elected Popular Front government, yet here was the French government abetting the fascist enemy. At the same time, the authority of the PCF was considerably enhanced in the eyes of left-wing intellectuals when the Soviet Union came to the support of a beleaguered Spanish Republic. From this point forward, disillusionment was inevitable. Total disillusionment was momentarily avoided when the government raised the spectre of international war as an excuse for its actions. Whether Renoir personally conceded this excuse, I cannot be sure. In January 1937 *La Marseillaise* was being planned, at first as a film on Jean Juarès, who had argued that it was peace, and peace alone, that was truly revolutionary. From February through April 1937, Renoir did direct the pacific and conciliatory *La Grande Illusion*, which attacks the great illusion that war can be for the good of man. And he continued the Left's attack on Hitler, Mussolini, and Franco, and the battle against anti-Semitism and fascism on the home front in the sixty-odd articles he wrote for *Ce Soir* from 4 March 1937 to 4 November 1938. It is a measure of Renoir's importance to the Party that he was given this journalistic assignment by Louis Aragon, then the editor of the PCF daily.

All of this activity is evidence of Renoir's steadfast commitment to the antifascist and reformist politics of the period. But for an artist, commitment should mean more than articulating correct political views, it should reveal itself in his art, in the subject matter of that art, and, if he is a revolutionary artist, in the extent to which he has revolutionized his artistic forms. And in that sense, on the evidence of his filmic practice—despite one radical film work—Renoir is not a revolutionary artist. But then, the aspirations of the Popular Front were not revolutionary either. The Front defended democracy to an alliance of the working class and the bourgeoisie rather than promote revolution as the antidote to fascism and the worst privileges of capitalism. And the Parti Communiste Français acceded to this compromise; there is no reason to suppose Renoir would have tendered his support had it not. Historical conditions of the 1935-1938 period brought to political focus the investigative sociology of his work of the beginning of the decade. If there appears to be some contradiction between the radicalism of Renoir's extracinematic activities during the late thirties and the milder temper of his films—did Renoir install *himself* as one of the excoriated "sons of the bourgeoisie"?—that is because the films offer us forms of social perception rather than conceptual analysis. The films represent what it feels like to live in and through the social relations and historical conditions operating in society at a given moment. These films do not at all represent "reality"; they signify—to use a phrase I have used before—the mythified desiderata of the collective Left. Excepting *La Vie est à nous*, for tactical reasons they carry their ideological intervention to a fundamentally bourgeois audience—"the public of the exclusive cinemas"—whereas the writings and extracinematic activities were carried through PCF organs to predominately working-class audiences. Why and how the films might function in this way will be clear from an analysis of the reformist ideology of so popular a bourgeois fiction as *La Grande Illusion*. As Renoir had said himself, the public that guarantees the commercial success of a film is a bourgeois public, and *La Grande Illusion* was handsomely produced by Réalisation d'Art Cinématographique fully expecting a profitable return from that public. By all accounts, its première on 4 June 1937, at the Marivaux Cinema, Paris, and subsequent exhibition history in London and New York did not disappoint the producers. I do not wish the foregoing remarks to carry the least note of regret that Renoir's work was not different than it is, for his films represent an inestimable contribution to our grasp of the social function of cinema during the thirties in France.

La Grande Illusion is very much a Frontist film, "a documentary on the condition of society at a given moment," as Renoir described it. And this moment is 1937, of course, not the period of its historical setting during the First World War. *La Grande Illusion* tends to be the most widely admired of Renoir's films (the fifth greatest film of all time according to an international jury of 117 critics at the Brussels World's Fair in 1958), but I cannot help thinking that this admiration does the film an injustice, or rather, depends upon a misreading. This film, perhaps more than any other directed by Renoir during the thirties, is subject to that commonplace liability of auteurism that reads the man through the work (or the work in the man). By universalizing the work and essentializing the man the conclusion has been reached that Renoir does not take sides, that in his all-embracing humanity he rises above politics:

Renoir's work shuffles the cards and teaches us no longer to judge, to understand that one can understand nothing. An example: Dien Bien Phu is a victory or a defeat depending on your point of view.[18]

War is only a mishap that turns out to be a little more serious than this permanent game of charades.[19]

Had these remarks been uttered in 1937 they would have thrown Renoir into a dumb rage, for they utterly dehistoricize *La Grande Illusion* and create a fictional identity for Renoir that denies him any capacity for moral responsibility. As foolish as such comments may now appear, they nevertheless reflect and abet a popular opinion of Renoir and of this film. But *La Grande Illusion* remains an openly political film. Those who banned the film— Goebbels ("cinematographic enemy number one"), Mussolini (an "anti-heroic" film), Paul-Henri Spaak (the Belgian foreign minister and brother of Charles Spaak, Renoir's co-writer), the Vichy government ("demoralizing")—those who supported it—Roosevelt ("All the democracies of the world must see this film")— knew its political worth.

What film criticism must accept is that qualities for which Renoir the man is generally praised in regard to this film—his much celebrated fraternity and internationalism—were produced by the Popular Front. In fact, there is no useful evidence that these are qualities of character at all; rather, they are themes, themes authored by history. They are not "natural" to Renoir or inherent in his personality (although it is usually assumed they are).[20] Where do they appear in the work before 1935 or

[18] François Truffaut, "Comme il y a vingt ans: *La Grande Illusion* de Jean Renoir est d'une brûlante actualité," *Arts*, no. 691 (14 October 1958), p. 7.

[19] Claude Beylie, *Jean Renoir: le spectacle, la vie* (Paris: Editions Seghers, 1975), p. 56.

[20] In his later years Renoir has given comfort to the idealists (perhaps having listened to them in the first place), despite the uneven evidence of the films: "My chief aim [in *La Grande Illusion*] was the one which I have been pursuing ever since I started to make films—to express the common humanity of men." This remark appears in *My Life and My Films* (New York: Atheneum, 1974), p. 148.

after 1937—except, not surprisingly, in the special documentary *Salute to France* (made for the United States Office of War Information in 1944), and possibly in the privileged moment on the farm at the conclusion of *Le Caporal épinglé* (1962)? Perhaps, too, because we are removed from the period, we overemphasize the film's internationalism (our late twentieth-century idealism!) at the expense of its theme of class, when both should be considered together because both were a part of Frontist ideology.

How does *La Grande Illusion* read the historical situation of 1937? There were 349 feature films made in France from 1936 to 1938; 99 of these were produced in 1937. Not all feature productions saw the contemporary situation as Renoir's film did. Contrary to the pacifism of *La Grande Illusion*, for example, Marcel L'Herbier's *Veille d'armes* (1935) was openly militarist and advocated a French arms buildup. During the middle and late thirties L'Herbier was to the political Right what Renoir was to the Left. Other films and film makers (directors, producers) evidently thought as Renoir did, if more crudely. Gérard Talon, who has provided the production figures for the period, draws attention to Léo Joannon's *Alerte en Méditerranée* (1938) as a film that advances a theme of international cooperation based on the fraternity and political unanimity displayed by three naval commanders.[21]

Although the thematic concerns of *La Grande Illusion* are very much a product of contemporary history, it is also true that the first rough plot of the film as a series of attempted escapes from First World War prison camps came from Renoir's chance meeting with an old acquaintance in 1934. During the filming of *Toni* at Martigues, Renoir met General Pinsard, a World War I French flying ace who had saved Renoir's plane from being downed by German fighters. They had celebrated Pinsard's victory with a champagne dinner, an elegant custom that is nicely

[21] Gérard Talon, "Le Cinéma du Front Populaire," *Cinéma 75*, no. 194 (January 1975), pp. 34-56.

recalled for Von Rauffenstein's celebration in the second scene of *La Grande Illusion*. On the occasion of their renewed acquaintance in 1934 Pinsard told Renoir of his seven successful escapes from German prisoner-of-war camps. Fictionalized as "Les Evasions du Capitaine Maréchal," Pinsard's exploits were the basis of the first scenario. For other elements of the film Renoir also drew upon personal reminiscence: Maréchal's first encounter with De Boeldieu is a reenactment of Renoir's meeting with a condescending staff officer whom he was assigned to take on a reconnaissance mission; the droll scene around the costume crate as the men discuss the wartime change in women's fashions was prompted by the remembered astonishment caused by a visit to Renoir in hospital from his sister-in-law in 1915; Gabin, as Maréchal, is said to be wearing Renoir's uniform of the French Flying Corps in the first scene of the film; and the officer's mess in that scene is apparently a reconstruction of Renoir's own.[22] If I cite certain elements of the film as having been drawn from Renoir's experience, that is because I want to say that while knowledge of indebtedness to personal reminiscence may have antiquarian value, it does not contrive to make *La Grande Illusion* a more personal film. What matters, finally, is the use to which these elements have been put, both thematically and stylistically, and that is largely due to forces beyond the author's intervention:

> The language and devices a writer finds to hand are already saturated with certain ideological modes of perception, certain codified ways of interpreting reality; and the extent to which he can modify or remake those languages depends on more than his personal genius. It depends on whether at that point in history, 'ideology' is such that they must and can be changed.[23]

[22] These bits of reminiscence may be found in *My Life and My Films*, pp. 151, 160, and *Renoir, My Father* (Boston: Little, Brown, 1962), pp. 21-22.

[23] Terry Eagleton, *Marxism and Literary Criticism* (London: Methuen, 1976), pp. 26-27.

What began, in 1934, as a story of a succession of escapes from German prison camps became, in 1937, a Frontist-inspired ideologically determined perception of experience. With the passage of time and the absence of a context the present-day spectator is unaware of the processes of selection and exclusion that went into the construction of *La Grande Illusion*. Could we be informed of these processes—in part by viewing a great many films contemporaneous with *La Grande Illusion*—we would see the text/pretext of the film anew and be able to grasp its ideological imperative and its placement of the spectator-subject in 1937. One can note, however, that certain generic as well as thematic emphases may result from specific ideological positions. New generic developments, with their attendant thematic emphases, embody new perceptions of social reality. Gérard Talon has ascertained that, given the political issues of the period, between 1936 and 1938 a love story had a 63 percent chance of interesting the public if it took place during the First World War, in a military setting, and raised problems concerning national duty. Two examples cited—neither of which I have seen—are *Paix sur le Rhin* (1938) by Jean Choux and *Marthe Richard* (1937) by Raymond Bernard. This last was made at Joinville directly before *La Grande Illusion* and starred Erich von Stroheim as a Prussian officer! As the sets were being struck for the one film, those for *La Grande Illusion* were put into place. Von Stroheim went directly from working with Bernard to working with Renoir, causing Renoir to reshape the part of Von Rauffenstein during production of *La Grande Illusion*. Can Renoir and Charles Spaak have been oblivious to the potential of the generic factor in their story? They certainly managed to meet all the criteria, even to the love interest, usually the most maligned sequence in *La Grande Illusion*.

Arguably, however, this concluding sequence at Elsa's mountain farm, far from being extraneous, is the sequence most crucial to the ideological value of the entire film. It is the most intense emotionally, while avoiding all sentimentality. Certainly, it is

one of the very great sequences in all of Renoir's work, especially
the scene on Christmas Eve, a scene so moving because it is
hallowed by the unforced religious symbolism of four lives
shared across boundaries of class, nationality, language, culture,
faith, sex, and age. This particular scene begins with a close-up
of the little model of the stable at Bethlehem, which Rosenthal
(Marcel Dalio) has carefully fashioned from sticks and straw,
potatoes, and bits of string, until the camera tracks back to open
up the space and reveal the three adults clustered around in
admiration. Beginning a scene with a close-up, as Renoir so
often does, invariably has the function of establishing the object
thus tightly framed as a symbol that seeds the meaning of the
entire scene to follow. And yet the symbolism remains understated, because Renoir never cuts but always tracks from this
initial position of the camera so that the object that introduces
the scene is always literalized in and by the surrounding space.

The very first shot of *La Grande Illusion* begins on a close-
up of a gramophone scratching out a popular melody, followed
by a tilt up to a flyer in uniform singing "Frou-frou," followed
again by a pan across the room as his attention is distracted. We
know we are in an officer's mess during the First World War.
However, as Maréchal looks for an opportunity to ride to town
to see "Josephine" (his girl?) but is told he must go out on a
mission, what strikes us is the conflict between civilian desires
and military necessities, which is not only the keynote of the
scene, established by the initial surprising juxtaposition of the
popular song and this uniformed officer, but which shall be a
keynote of the entire film.

Sometimes Renoir uses both the aural and visual potential of
this device for continuity through several scenes. The opening
four scenes of *La Règle du jeu* all begin with either the sound
or the sight of a radio carrying the broadcast from the airport,
symbolically and literally showing the problems of communi-
cation in love and friendship between the film's principal characters. As for the scene in the farmhouse on Christmas Eve in

La Grande Illusion, we would be hard pressed to miss the meaning of this Christian festival, which urges peace on earth and good-will towards men, in an antiwar film. Emotionally the scene is accepted as true; it has an unquestionable authority. What we respond to, I think, is the need that human beings have for one another, a need most ardently expressed in Maréchal's faltering efforts to articulate "Lotte hat blaue Augen." And the scene is carried very simply, without flourishes of camera or cutting, by the characters who have relaxed for the first time in the film, and by the setting, our first civilian environment in the entire film. One might even point to a natural clumsiness here that enhances the scene: the derailment of the gramophone; the awkwardness of the movements of Gabin and Dita Parlo (as Elsa) when they pass through the door of Lotte's room to wake her for the surprise, and, later, as they embrace; the makeshift crèche; Lotte's desire to eat the potato-carving of baby Jesus. The sequence as a whole conveys an extraordinary sense of well-being, and Renoir is at his most effective in shooting through doors and windows to link the domesticity of the farm with the freshness of the open landscape. We have a sense of space, a sense of liberation, that we have not had in the film until now. Maréchal stretches at his ease against mountain and sky, and we recall his incarceration in the filthy cell of the first prison camp. Rosenthal lounges in a chair while he unassumedly teaches Lotte to count to ten, and we recall his earlier defensiveness about his race when providing sumptuous meals for his fellow prisoners.

Of course, the sequence on the mountain farm has been prepared for by the film; it has not been stumbled upon by an accident of the scenario or unmotivated design. Nor does it produce its effect on us by achieving some "human" level beyond the questions of class and militarism with which the film as a whole deals. Its tenderness has been earned. The tenderness of this idyll is the best comment on war and class in the entire film, for no other sequence more effectively judges the futility of war, the stupidity of national enmities, or the burden of class distinctions. One assumes that this sequence is sufficiently convincing so as to have been available to contemporary audiences as a moral—and through that an ideological—appeal. In the context of 1937, for example, one might appreciate the force of this appeal when news reached France that fascist planes had destroyed Guernica. But that is not all there is to it. To a very great extent the conviction of the sequence depends upon its emotionality, and, as we shall see, this emotionality is designed to obscure the historical reality that lies outside the text/pretext of the film.[24]

A bad director would have ended his film here, on the mountain farm. (A mediocre director would have ended it with the escape of Maréchal and Rosenthal from the fortress and have thoroughly enobled De Boeldieu at their expense.) Maréchal and Rosenthal must leave the farm, partly because the film would otherwise fall into bathos and false optimism, a conclusion Renoir failed to avoid in *Les Bas-Fonds*, his previous film. But Renoir successfully avoids the charge of escapism here, as he did with the justification of the cooperative in *Le Crime de M. Lange* by the leave-taking of Lange and Valentine to their qualified freedom in exile in the film's epilogue. Above all, Maréchal and Rosenthal must leave the farm because they would be deserters if they did not, and political circumstances could not permit that. (The PCF, as a matter of policy, and Renoir were firmly patriotic.) If Maréchal and Rosenthal were to remain, their desertion would be an idealist renunciation of history on Renoir's part. To go on is to plunge back "into" history, and an acknowledgement of history as process. The Parti Communiste Français and the Popular Front *exist*. Maréchal and Rosenthal choose history and choose the possibility of social transformation. One can now understand why the ending originally proposed

[24] As an added note, this haven of peace and good-will, the mountain farm, is unquestionably in the disputed territory of Alsace. The point could not have been lost on contemporary audiences.

for the film was revised. Maréchal and his companion (Dolette, in the first scenario) were to leave the farm, successfully make their way to Switzerland, and agree to meet again on the first Christmas after the war at Maxim's. The final scene was to show a restaurant crowded with celebrants, but for a reserved table in the centre of the room with two empty chairs. Emphatically pessimistic, this ending must have been rejected as ideologically unacceptable, for it seems not to admit that the course of history can be changed. With the tentative promise offered by the ending that we do have, the interlude on the mountain farm *is* an idyll, because the coda which follows allows that it represents what one would like to be but what may well never be. Maréchal will probably never return, despite his expressed intention.

Again, this sequence represents what *is* and what is not *yet*. Is it Renoir's felt expression of that spot of (future) time for the social harmony envisaged by the Popular Front? Certainly there is nothing like it to be found in Renoir's other works of this period. Not only by its special feeling do we know this sequence for an idyll; we are continually reminded of its fragility. The war, the world, waits outside. A passing German soldier stops at the farmhouse window to ask directions; Elsa commemorates her husband and her brothers by reciting a sad litany of German "victories"; four empty chairs are upturned on an empty table; Maréchal admonishes Lotte's desire to eat the potato-carving of baby Jesus with a "Streng verboten" in recollection of the guards' refrain at their first prison camp; the fate of De Boeldieu is wondered at; Rosenthal still knows the reality of anti-Semitism by thinking aloud of Jesus as his "racial brother" on Christmas Eve. The authority with which the sequence is handled holds out its real ideological worth to the film, and it is not come by fortuitously.

When, in the film's last, distant shot we see Maréchal and Rosenthal plunging knee-deep through the snow across that illusive border into Switzerland, after the idyll on the farm, they now carry with them a better sense of what they are fighting for (isn't that what the film has been about?), and by implication (for the audience, at least), what they are fighting against:

> *Maréchal*: I'll come back for Elsa.
> *Rosenthal*: You love her?
> *Maréchal*: I believe, yes. However, allowing for the fact that we make it, you'll return to your squadron, and me, to my battery. We're going to take up the struggle. Like our buddies, we've got to end this whore of a war ... hoping that it will be the last.
> *Rosenthal*: Ah! you're kidding yourself! Go on! To get back to reality: if we come across a patrol, what are we going to do?[25]

Ironically, for all the film's advocacy of breaking down certain borders (of nationality, race, culture, language, faith), it is a border that saves Maréchal and Rosenthal. The German patrol that spots them is ordered not to shoot because they have crossed over into Switzerland, although the precise boundary line between one country and another is invisible beneath the uniform blanket of snow. The humanly manufactured reality of borders is reinstated, however, as a last hedge against the film's optimism about the possibilities of social transformation.

What Maréchal and Rosenthal are fighting against has been represented to us by those military aristocrats De Boeldieu and Von Rauffenstein. De Boeldieu and Von Rauffenstein may not be villains in a deliberate sense, but then they are not exactly harmless either. Louis XVI and Robert de la Chesnaye are treated similarly in *La Marseillaise* and *La Règle du jeu* respectively. Evidence of a sympathetic treatment of all of these characters does not preclude a judgement of their class identities: "Good manners, even chivalry, do not excuse a massacre."[26] De Boeldieu and Von Rauffenstein both display the obduracy and

---

[25] Jean Renoir, *La Grande Illusion* (Paris: Balland, 1974), pp. 200-201.

[26] Quoted by Sesonske, *Jean Renoir*, in the headnote to his chapter on *La Grande Illusion*, p. 282.

intransigence of their class. This is clear, I think, from the way in which their lives and behaviours are so meticulously represented in the film. Everything that serves to identify who and what they are marks their separation from the motivations of Maréchal and Rosenthal. And between the two opposing pairs of officers is the unbridgeable gulf of incomprehension. In terms of behaviour, the class difference of De Boeldieu and Von Rauffenstein is established by their self-conscious display of style, of life lived as a form of spectacle. Von Rauffenstein is the more exotic character, quartered in the chapel at Wintersborn with its disproportionately huge crucifix, surrounded by his whips and spurs (for what purposes?) and a copy of Casanova's *Memoirs* (for what fantasy?), tending his solitary geranium. White gloves cover his burned hands, while a chin-brace, corset, and silver plates in his knee and head hold his fractured body together. What an astonishing representative of the Prussian military aristocracy! His disdain for Maréchal and Rosenthal, those products of the French Revolution, is open, while his anti-Semitism is barely veiled. His counterpart, De Boeldieu, is less flamboyant, although no less formal and aloof from the Maréchals and Rosenthals of this world ("Je dis 'vous' à ma femme, et 'vous' à ma mère"). With his monocle and his fastidiousness, his request for an armchair and his preference for English tobacco, his mannered elegance seems absurdly out of place in the milieu of the film's prison camps. English is the lingua franca of the European aristocracy, and that is the language De Boeldieu and Von Rauffenstein speak as they discuss horses or women they have known, separately or shared, in the pleasure spots of Europe before the war. Cutting across national differences, these are the cultural preoccupations of their class, which allows that they have more in common with each other than with the likes of a Maréchal or a Rosenthal.

Perhaps it is the very frivolity of their lives before the war, lives sustained by inherited privilege, that explains why war gives these career officers their only purposes. Without war they have no useful function. And this film does not want war. Both can acknowledge, therefore, that the end of this war will be the end of the Rauffensteins and the Boeldieus, although the latter seems more certain or more resigned to the prospect than the former, perhaps because he has been confined with the anti-militaristic Maréchal through several prison camps and through him has been able to glimpse the future. (It is not, of course, irrelevant that such a speculation on the part of the film may be a wish-fulfilling aspect of its ideological function, and in retrospect part of its historical naiveté.) Fittingly, the last prison camp, the medieval fortress of Wintersborn, will be their mausoleum. It will be the architectural symbol of their class and its military necessities, of their tradition, their historical privilege, and their culture. It is everything they represent, as the farmhouse rep-resents the civilian, utopian desires of Maréchal and Rosenthal. Removed from combat by the fortunes of war and the design of the film, the one a prisoner and the other a policeman, De Boeldieu and Von Rauffenstein have nothing left to them but their rituals of self-conscious style. On this score, Von Rauffen-stein's act of clipping the flower from the unique geranium in an environment of ivy and nettles indicates his self-absorbtion, his romantic self-pity even, just as De Boeldieu's ostentatious "sacrifice" for Maréchal and Rosenthal indicates his. These are their private theatricals. The ruse devised by De Boeldieu to effect the escape of Maréchal and Rosenthal is very obviously produced by him as a spectacle. He first bathes himself and then prepares his costume by brushing his uniform and washing his white gloves. This ceremony is marvellously detailed by Renoir in a number of long takes in order to maximize the sense of De Boeldieu's creation of a proper persona. When he does perform his little *divertissement* on the ramparts of the castle, it is to the sound of music provided by the fife and in the glare of the spotlights obligingly provided by Von Rauffenstein. Before De Boeldieu falls, shot by Von Rauffenstein, he makes one last exaggerated show of looking at his watch to climax the success of his performance. Neither Maréchal nor Rosenthal, who do not witness this display, understands at all why De Boeldieu is prepared to risk his life. They take for altruism what is in fact a self-interested act. In the first place, De Boeldieu makes it clear that for him sentiment has no importance. And in the second place he admits to Von Rauffenstein that his death is a "good solution" because it is in a manner of his own choosing and consistent with the sense of style about his life. "Duty is duty," both De Boeldieu and Von Rauffenstein say, and they will play out the imperatives of that code to its ruthless conclusion. (Contrast Maréchal's "illusions," his naiveté about soldiering, his sentimental attachments.)

I do not see how we can fail to associate their class and the attitudes of that class with militarism, just as audiences were meant to do in 1937. In this regard the First World War setting does not function simply as an accident of generic determination; it has ideological value, too. The film's First World War setting allows that its "reading" of the social reality of 1937 has been historically produced. The career officers of 1914 who orchestrated that carnage known as "the war to end all wars" are the forebearers of the right-wing militarists opposed to the pacific and antifascist policies of the Popular Front. Similarly, *La Marseillaise* re-presents the Revolution of 1792, thereby allowing the work to stand as a *film-à-clé* for the aspirations of the Popular Front, while acknowledging that those aspirations have been produced by history. With this emphasis upon class differences in *La Grande Illusion*—especially the militarism of the one as opposed to the domestic, civilian wants of the other—rather than upon national enmities, the film's perception is ideologically consistent with the position of the Left in 1937.

La Grande Illusion did not, however, prevent World War II: "In 1936 [*sic*] I made a picture named *La Grande Illusion* in which I tried to express all my deep feelings for the cause of peace.... Three years later the war broke out."[27] In some respects

[27] Jean Renoir, in *Film: Book 2*, ed. Robert Hughes (New York: Grove Press, 1962), p. 183.

the film's naiveté is now patent. Not only did it fail to prevent World War II—one did not expect it to do so all by itself—it failed to analyze correctly the political realities of 1937 which abetted that war. Maréchal and Rosenthal, the working man and the new bourgeois, are shown, with qualified optimism, to be the inheritors of the earth. In terms of their real social relations they should be class enemies, but the emotionality of the sequence on the mountain farm especially manages to obscure their historical antagonism. Nowhere in the film does Renoir show class struggle; he shows only class differences. He clearly identifies the aristocratic career officers, De Boeldieu and Von Rauffenstein, but blurs the class distinction between Maréchal and Rosenthal. If we were to give the matter some thought we should realize that Rosenthal, the banker's son, the *nouveau riche*, who boasts of his family's acquisition of tapestries, paintings, game-parks, lands, and châteaux, is the historical successor in material terms to De Boeldieu's inherited rights, privileges, and social standing. (A telling detail: above his bed at Wintersborn Rosenthal has posted reproductions of Botticelli, while De Boeldieu has his photographs of racehorses.) It is the power and influence of this new mercantilism that will finally sound the death knell of the old European aristocracy. In an extraordinary performance, Marcel Dalio again plays Robert de la Chesnaye in *La Règle du jeu*, that weak representative of the French *haute bourgeoisie* whose condemnable complacency and self-interest would welcome the compromises with Hitler in 1938 and 1939. The ideological value carried by the "universal" Christian symbolism and the strongly felt appeal of the idyll on the mountain farm in *La Grande Illusion* is that the transformation of society can be effected by the alliance of a Maréchal and a Rosenthal. Both the cultural codes at work in the sequence and Renoir's species of illusionist practice intend to signify the timelessness of our common humanity and the essentiality of our human nature while obscuring real, historically determined conditions of social existence in 1937.

But inasmuch as this is a bourgeois fiction addressed to a bourgeois public—perhaps that is why there are no infantrymen, only officers in the film—the idyll of the text fits the pretext of the film's Frontist-inspired role. The alliance of Maréchal and Rosenthal is the sort of compromise that potential class enemies were asked to make during the Popular Front period. International class solidarity (bourgeois and proletarian) would prove, it was believed, to be stronger than national interests, and thereby prevent the oncoming war that was identified with fascist militarism. Renoir's confidence in the artificiality of national frontiers was the greatest and most naive of *his* illusions. Intraclass solidarity proved to be vertical, not horizontal, as national interests dominated all other considerations in the European conflagration that followed *La Grande Illusion* by two-and-one-half years. In retrospect, we may have the greatest emotional sympathy for Renoir's faith, but we cannot erase from our historical consciousness the knowledge that it was (and is) hopelessly inadequate. Renoir's film may rise far above the worst of the genre in this or any other period, but it cannot escape the ideological determinations of the moment. Nevertheless, if it seems probable that Renoir—like everyone else—showed more faith than analytical understanding of the complex issues involved, that is not to undermine his degree of commitment to the aspirations of the Popular Front.

These aspirations suffered a number of setbacks through the latter half of 1937 and on into 1938. Blum was forced to resign in June 1937, and Camille Chautemps formed a Radical Party, do-nothing government. The noninterventionist policy towards Spain was preserved, while economic concessions were granted that permitted capital to regain the footing it had lost in 1936. The ruin of the Popular Front was a step away. In this regard the fate of *La Marseillaise* now seems premonitory. It began as a film about a revolution for a revolution, and it was to be produced in a revolutionary way. Organised by Ciné-liberté, production was to be financed by public subscription and carried through with the voluntary participation of the Confédération Générale du Travail and the most celebrated cast and crew in Europe.[28] As "a film about events contributing to the fall of the monarchy," *La Marseillaise* would offer a "reading" of French history in which certain events of 1792 were treated in such a way as to parallel directly circumstances and conditions of 1937.

But just as the original production initiatives collapsed, resulting in conventional methods of financing, distribution and exhibition, so the treatment turned out to be conciliatory rather than revolutionary. Shot between October and November 1937, its advocacy seems to me no different than that of *La Grande Illusion*. *La Marseillaise* was released at a time (February 1938) when the crest of the wave for a radical transformation of French society had passed. Still, as one would expect, the Right attacked the film venomously and the Left defended it. But there was a perceptible lack of exuberance in the Left's defense, as though its spokesmen felt bound only by reasons of affiliation. Worse, the Left itself was not solid.[29] Henri Jeanson, in particular, a staunch defender of *La Vie est à nous*, saw the writing on the wall. In an article entitled "*La Marseillaise*, or the Deceits of Stalin," published in *La Flèche de Paris* on 19 February 1938, Jeanson attacked Renoir as a dupe of Stalinism, despite the best intentions of his film.[30] The huge press elicited by *La Marseillaise* is just as interesting as the film itself, and perhaps a better index to its ideological value than its text.

Dissipation of the focussed energies of the Left continued without check. On 15 January 1938, dozens of French intellectuals, Renoir among them, issued a desperate plea to the government to respect the popular will expressed in the 1936 elections. Camille Chautemp's eventual reply was his resignation in

[28] Details concerning financing and personnel may be found in my *Jean Renoir: A Guide to References and Resources*, pp. 108-112.

[29] See "Il y a 35 ans *La Marseillaise*," ed. Claude Gauteur, *Image et Son*, no. 268 (February 1973), pp. 66 and 68.

[30] Reprinted in *Image et Son*, no. 268 (February 1973), pp. 66-70.

March 1938. At this very moment Hitler marched into Austria. Since this was the first unequivocal challenge to a nation's sovereignty by a fascist power, Hitler's aggressive intentions should have been unmistakable. Demoralisation was swift, however, as Blum twice tried to form a credible ministry, appealing to the extreme Right and the extreme Left for support, and failing both times. On 13 April 1938, Edouard Daladier succeeded in forming a government of appeasement with a Radical Party ministry. And despite criticism from the Communists, its foreign policy towards the reality of fascism in Spain, Germany, Italy, and Portugal was passive. France, the left recognized, had evaded its responsibilities.

In this climate of disillusionment Renoir shot *La Bête humaine* in August and September 1938. With *La Bête humaine*, the contradiction between Renoir's practice as a film maker and his avowed political position in the press is suddenly real and divisive. *La Bête humaine* is not a Frontist film. In this respect it is as anomalous a work as *Partie de campagne*. From the social determination of character Renoir has regressed to the individualist psychological fatality of Jacques Lantier (Jean Gabin). The uncontrollable seizures that lead him to commit acts of violence against women are produced by the alcoholism of his forefathers. So far as the film is concerned, Lantier's class definition and his occupation as an engine-driver are socially irrelevant to his psychological state. The film's principal setting, the railway yards at Le Havre, is atmospheric rather than exemplary of a social condition. *La Bête humaine* has more in common with the romantic fatalism conjured up by Carné–Prévert in *Quai des brumes* (1938) and *Le Jour se lève* (1939), or by Duvivier in *Pepe le moko* (1937), than it does with the reform-minded productions of the Popular Front. In all four films the protagonist is played by Jean Gabin, a doomed, languishing figure, filmed in the still pool of life's shadows, caught in a desperate love affair with no prospects. These are the films, not *La Grande Illusion*, that secured the Gabin persona of the thirties as a mythified *idea* of the working-class type, an idea that became a vehicle for pathos rather than the possibilities of social change.

The place of *La Bête humaine* in this minor genre of the thirties might be confirmed by its première on 23 December 1938 before the most distinguished audience of statesmen and stars that Paris could muster, followed by a highly successful run of four months. But on the evidence of his writings from the period, Renoir did not see his film in the context I have suggested at all. In the first place, he attacked *Quai des brumes* as a reactionary film, thereby disavowing any similarities with *La Bête humaine*. And in an article for *L'Avant-garde* on 6 October, 1938, Renoir defended his working-class comrades, the railway workers, against the disrespect shown their métier by the ignorant journalists assigned to cover the making of the film.[31] On 15 December 1938, in *Les Cahiers de la Jeunesse*, Renoir spoke of his film in very strong political terms:

> It is a revolutionary subject, since it leads to the conclusion that individuals living in better conditions would act better. ... It is a refutation of the facile reactionary theory which supports the convention that human beings are immutable, destined to act in a certain way, and that it is useless to attempt anything towards their amelioration. You are born poor, you will remain poor. You are born rich, you will remain rich. There will always be the happy and the unhappy, and equality is a foolish word.[32]

But this seems to me special pleading, for an examination of the film itself and the motivations of its protagonist does not lend support to Renoir's opinion of its subject. About all that one may say of it in a Frontist vein is to note with irony that among its successes the government could count the semi-nationalised amalgamation of the French railway companies. I cannot ra-

---

[31] Reprinted in *Image et Son*, no. 315 (March 1977), pp. 26-27.

[32] Jean Renoir, "Cinéma," *Cahiers de la Jeunesse*, no. 17 (15 December 1938), p. 24.

tionalize Renoir's evident contradiction. It is true that the subject was proposed to Renoir as a commercial venture, and that he took it on at the last minute after it had been taken away from Jean Grémillon by the Hakim brothers. Whether Renoir was privately aware of this contradiction between his political advocacy and his filmic practice, I cannot say. The evidence suggests that he was not. In any case, there is no argument in support of a claim for the ideological continuity of *La Bête humaine* with Renoir's other films of this period.

Still, that is *not* an argument for the film's neglect; I simply do not wish the context in which it should be discussed to be misunderstood. The film's merits—and they are considerable—do invite comparison with the films of the period by Carné-Prévert and Duvivier. *La Bête humaine* does not suffer in the comparison. Its narrative structure is tightly controlled, its acting is superb, and certain passages in the film, notably the opening sequence of the train journey from Paris to Le Havre and the juxtaposition of Séverine's murder with the railwaymen's ball, surpass in invention the best work of other directors. If Renoir's films of the thirties, of the Popular Front period especially, express what it feels like to live in and through the social relations and historical conditions operating in society at a given moment, then perhaps the peculiar value of *La Bête humaine* for our immediate purposes is its (inadvertent?) indication that the moment of revolution, certainly the hoped-for moment of significant social change, had passed for good. The making of *La Bête humaine* coincides with the collapse of the government of the Popular Front and the ultimate disappointment of the hopes nurtured by the intellectual Left. Towards the end of October 1938, Daladier turned on the PCF and abandoned the Popular Front alliance for good.

While *La Bête humaine* was being edited, Renoir took time out to write his next-to-last column for *Ce Soir* on 7 October 1938. He had not written for the paper since 3 September, but presumably he was roused to speak once again by the topic:

Munich. The article is entitled "Ah! qu'on est fier d'être français quand on contemple la colonne!" ("Ah! one is proud to be French when one thinks of the backbone!"). Satirical and bitter, Renoir compares the deal made at Munich to white-slave traffic, and concludes, prophetically:

> Thus the Germans will enter the cities of the Sudetenland. Will our papers publish the news, as they did for Vienna, with photographs of the choice jokes the Hitlerites will not miss the opportunity of playing on the Jews of these regions? Will we see, once again, old people on their knees in the mud washing the sidewalks? Women obliged to walk about carrying vile placards? In brief, will we once again be indirect and distant witnesses to this Nazi farce which imposes itself so willingly and so delicately on the vanquished?[33]

These remarks suggest that Renoir is no longer the advocate of pacifism he once was. His rejection of the Munich appeasement was a singular stand, since the majority of Frenchmen and the majority of left-wing intellectuals did not share his dismay, despite the visible hypocrisy of the French government after its continual assurances through the summer and fall of that fateful year that it would stand by Czechoslovakia and concede nothing to Hitler's demands on behalf of the Sudeten Nazi Party. Among France's political parties, the PCF was alone in its unanimous opposition to the four-power agreement at Munich, which brought the Party charges of treason and the renewed venom of the Right. When the Munich agreement was debated in the Chamber of Deputies, one Radical, one Socialist, and the seventy-three Communists voted against the motion, a stand that helped Daladier justify his denunciation of the PCF, dissolve the Popular Front alliance, and exclude the Communists and the Socialists from a new right-of-centre government. Whatever the

---

[33] Renoir, *Ecrits 1926-1971*, p. 178.

cost of betrayal—of self and others—popular relief that the European powers had averted another world war drowned the outcries of the Left. The *danse macabre* of European rejoicing at the Munich agreement made it impossible for the French Left to muster its former support. While the Popular Front collapsed, for the time being Renoir continued his personal association with the Parti Communiste Français. In line with the position of the Party during this period, Renoir affirmed his patriotism, notably in an article entitled "Souvenirs," published in *Le Point* in December 1938:

> I know that I am French and that I must work in an absolutely national vein. I know also that in doing this, and only in doing this, can I reach people from other nations and act for international understanding.[34]

On 27 January 1939, Renoir was in London, where he reaffirmed his nationalist stance to a meeting of the Association of Cine-Technicians, and to which he added:

> In parenthesis, I should like to say that circumstances may well arise—I need not particularize, we all know them only too well—in which I shall be forced to seek freedom in England.[35]

This, I believe, is the first premonition we have that Renoir would leave France. Following upon his skepticism over Munich, he certainly seems to have accepted the inevitability of war.

It was in the aftermath of Munich that Renoir planned *La Règle du jeu*, the film that concludes his first career as a film maker, that is, his actively political career. *La Règle du jeu* is a devastating response to the defeat of the Left's Popular Front idealism. That democratic idealism was dealt its final blow with the betrayal at Munich. After Spain, the Munich pact was Pelion

---

[34] Reprinted in Bazin, *Jean Renoir*, p. 158.
[35] "Jean Renoir Discusses His Past, Present, and Future," *The Cine-Technician* 4, no. 20 (March-April 1939), p. 178.

heaped on Ossa. Compromise had become cowardice. *La Règle du jeu* was the obituary of the hope for political and social change that had sustained Renoir and his many compatriots on the intellectual Left since 1935.

Renoir, however, was not about to resign himself to the failure of four years of commitment without a reply. Perhaps part of the reason *La Règle du jeu* is the masterwork of the French cinema of the thirties is because it is free of sectarian politics, although a profoundly political film. I do not believe that Renoir could have presented so bleak a portrait of his age were he not independent of party interests in making this film. The formation of his private production company, La Nouvelle Edition Française, a sort of French United Artists, in November and December of 1938, was the first indication that Renoir was severing his links with partisan politics. *La Règle du jeu* was the company's first and only production. And whatever may have been intended at the outset, when Renoir deposited a synopsis for a modern adaptation of Alfred de Musset's *Les Caprices de Marianne* with the Société des Auteurs in November 1938, the improvisational conditions under which the film was actually made allowed it to register the impact of the precipitous human and political catastrophe that was overtaking Europe at the beginning of 1939.

Although various states of the scenario for the film were sketched out during December and January, by the time shooting started on 22 February 1939, Renoir had dialogue and a shooting script for the first third of the film only, from the beginning at Le Bourget to the arrival of the house guests at La Colinière. Much of the casting was arranged at the last minute, including Paulette Dubost as Lisette, Renoir himself as Octave in default of his brother Pierre, Nora Gregor as Christine de la Chesnaye, and Mila Parèly as Geneviève de Marrast. On 26 January, while the French Chamber of Deputies was once again debating the government's noninterventionist policy, Barcelona fell to Franco, and Madrid followed on 27 March. In February, the French government officially extended diplomatic recognition to the Spanish government of General Franco. Renoir's bitterness over Munich received its justification on 15 March when Germany marched into Czechoslovakia. French mobilisation orders were subsequently issued during this month, although the cast and crew of *La Règle du jeu* were not affected directly. Film criticism will say that the confluence of political events surrounding the making of *La Règle du jeu* is not irrelevant to the shape and thrust of the resulting film. While suffering through a month of rain delays on location in the Sologne during this eventful March, Renoir took the opportunity to work on the remainder of his shooting script. At the end of the month he was forced to leave his second unit behind to film the hunt, and return to the Pathé Studios at Joinville to shoot interiors. Here new conceptions of character and last-minute changes to the script were made through April and early May. Renoir's extraordinary fastidiousness prolonged the production, as he frequently took countless takes of the same shot in which the actors did not repeat the same lines from one take to the next. Stills also exist for scenes that were shot but never printed. While Renoir argued over the budget for the film with his financial backers, and made continual revisions to his script, Italy invaded Albania on 7 April. And, as *La Règle du jeu* was being sent to the cutting room, Hitler talked Mussolini into a military alliance on 22 May.

Renoir had not been certain how his film should end and was prepared for two possibilities. In one, the film would conclude with the nighttime exterior of the leave-taking of Marceau (Julien Carette) and Octave, each to go his own way. Behind their last two-shot can be seen the terrace of the château. The second possibility, the conclusion as we have it, was La Chesnaye's apologetic eulogy for André Jurieu (Roland Toutain) from the steps of the château, followed by the General's closing remark, the shadows of the guests on the wall, and the rising music on the soundtrack. Finally, Marguerite Houllé, the editor, kept both scenes in the film. After five weeks in the cutting room, Houllé

cut together a picture 107 minutes in length, which was subsequently reduced to 97 minutes for its disastrous première on
7 July 1939.[36] The film was hooted at by opening-night audiences,
played for a mere three weeks, and received a thoroughly ambivalent press reception. Renoir's (ironic) disclaimer at the head
of the film, "Ce divertissement n'a pas la prétention d'être une
étude de moeurs et les personnages qu'il présente sont purement
imaginaires" ("This entertainment does not claim to be a study
of morals and the characters that it presents are entirely fictional"), appeased no one, least of all the French government,
which banned the film in October of 1939 as demoralising and
which reimposed the ban when the Nazis entered Paris in June
1940.[37]

The darkness falling over Europe is reflected in the savage
pessimism of *La Règle du jeu*. With hindsight, the complacency
and hypocrisy of the bourgeoisie represented in the film can be
taken as an indictment of its responsibility for the outbreak of
war. But a more productive reading of the film is one that sees
it as a summing up of the events and emotions of the years from
1935 on. Our knowledge, and the film's internal evidence that
it was made in the aftermath of Munich are sufficient proof that
La Règle du jeu represents a social reality that has been histor-

[36] Accounts of the production, distribution, and exhibition of the film (including my
own in *Jean Renoir: A Guide to References and Resources*), have given the running time
of the prerelease version as either 110 or 113 minutes and the time of the release print
as 100 minutes. Three additional shortened versions of 90, 85, and 80 minutes are also
presumed to have existed. Research into the exhibition history of the film that I have
recently conducted with Mark Freedman indicates that this information is quite erro-
neous. A comparison of prints and an analysis of the cuts made to the film at various
times have established that the film was never edited to 110 or 113 minutes. Marguerite
Houllé prepared a print that ran 107 minutes. At Gaumont's insistence, this fine cut
was reduced to 97 minutes for the film's première. After the war, the film played in
two other versions of approximately 86 and 80 minutes. So there were but four, not
five, versions of the film in existence. Prints made from the restored version released
in 1959 should run about 106 minutes since some missing picture track has never been
found.

[37] For a history of the production and exhibition of *La Règle du jeu*, see my *Jean
Renoir: A Guide to References and Resources*, pp. 114-127.

ically produced, but the film pessimistically allows that this social reality is no longer easily (peaceably?) transformed. The expectations that had been raised with the elections and reforms of 1936 were shattered. And in so far as the implementation of these expectations depended upon a politics of compromise and an economics of concession rather than radical change, perhaps the entrenchment of capital and the lassitude of decision-makers were inevitable. This I have no doubt Renoir realised, perhaps in what one must call an intuitive way, but he realised it nevertheless. What else can one say of a film that depicts a class, a society even, drawn in upon itself, and led by a master who declares that he does not want fences on his estate and he does not want rabbits either? That is not a tolerant, well-meaning attitude; it is an indecisive and irresponsible one. Such indecision is dangerous, even fatal. Renoir hit the truth when he gave out in an interview in January 1939, that *La Règle du jeu* was to be "a precise description of the bourgeoisie of our age." He later declared: "I knew the evil that was gnawing at my contemporaries"; and later he said: "It is a war film, and yet there is no reference to the war."[38] Justifiably, the film has elicited a great body of critical commentary.[39] I wish to make a few observations only. In particular, I want to note just how pessimistic a work it is.

On the surface, *La Règle du jeu* is a comedy of manners ("une étude de moeurs"), a kind of morality play on the veniality of human beings, regardless of their station in life. For this purpose, Renoir and his co-scenarists borrowed the structure and forms of five-act classical French comedy, with its exposition, complication, climax, reversal, and dénouement, including an entr'acte

[38] The sources of these three remarks are, respectively: an interview with Marguerite Bussot in *Pour Vous* for 25 January 1939, reprinted in Bazin, *Jean Renoir*, p. 184; an article in *Cahiers du Cinéma* 2, no. 8 (January 1952), p. 8; and, Renoir, *My Life and My Films*, p. 171.

[39] The most recent critical piece on the film is the long, sixty-page, final chapter of Sesonske's *Jean Renoir*, a discussion that is especially notable for its perceptive analysis of the characterizations in the film.

(the hunt sequence). They also borrowed the parallel star-crossed intrigues in the main plot and subplot (the Robert–Christine–André and Lisette–Schumacher–Marceau love triangles), costumed disguises appropriate to each personality (Christine as a Tyrolean maiden, Geneviève as a Spanish gypsy), mistaken identities (Christine for Lisette, André for Octave), and many of the character types for both masters and servants (a desperate lover, a fickle wife, a coquettish maid, a jealous husband, a parasitic go-between). The rules of this complexly orchestrated literary form are as conventional and as familiar as those for classical symphonic music. But in conflict with this stable theatrical inheritance in *La Règle du jeu* there is a generic uneasiness (as the film is now a comedy, now a slapstick farce, now a tragedy), and there are violent shifts in tone as we are wrenched from aching laughter to numb shock, in short, a frequently ruptured, occasionally discontinuous, and wholly unsettled narrative that threatens to explode the security of its borrowed frame. Our conventional expectations of the comedy of manners—presaged by the title itself—are continually interrupted, either by the juxtaposition of narrative incongruities (such as the savagery of the hunt prior to the hilarity of the fête), or by the effects of Renoir's conscious decision to cast against type (himself as Octave, Dalio as Robert, Gregor as Christine). This resistance to its ready-made structure, this refusal of neatness and predictability, allows the film to speak "out of character" as it were, to license the allusiveness of certain incidents (Octave's abortive performance before the imaginary orchestra on the steps of the château, for example), and the remarks of certain characters (in particular, the choric observations of Octave). The film thrives on just this tension between its traditional inheritance and its experimental excesses. It is these disturbances of the expected course of the text that led some reviewers in 1939 to judge *La Règle du jeu* a magnificent failure:

What is the impression that an audience retains after seeing this film? That it's a rich work—perhaps too rich—very complex and extremely intelligent from beginning to end; but that this very richness, this unmitigated humanity, this over-abundance of intentions has carried the film-maker too far and that he has not succeeded in controlling completely the magnificent material that he has himself invented. One might compare *La Règle du jeu* with one of those meandering streams, with many detours and wide recesses, that seems to provide us with the very image of nature's confusion.[40]

Evidence of neither narrative imperfection nor thematic confusion, this tension within the film's process of signification between tradition and innovation may be seen as an aspect of its modernism, for similar assaults on narrative expectation are at work from *The Waste Land* to *A bout du souffle*. The modernist experiment confirms a principle of structuralism: that how we see determines what we see. Changes in artistic form can mean new perceptions of social reality. The precise nature of the social existence of the film text (any film text) is very much a function of its formal properties. History speaks in *La Règle du jeu* not merely in *what* it documents of the disintegration of society in 1939, but in the *way* in which it documents it—in its entire signifying practice, in other words. At this historical moment, received modes of responding to and perceiving social experience are inadequate to the representation of the collapsing myths of bourgeois reality. Available forms would only produce available perceptions of experience. Therefore, the deformation of convention in *La Règle du jeu* signals, I believe, the interrogation of an ideologically determined mode of perception. The film's play with and against the structures of classical French comedy,

[40] Nino Frank's review of the film is reprinted and translated in Harcourt, *Six European Directors*, p. 90.

a form generated by and for the *haute bourgeoisie*, is a demonstration of the materialist notion that form *is* ideological. Unlike *La Grande Illusion, La Règle du jeu* is not a bourgeois fiction, precisely because it breaks trust with the bourgeoisie by exposing its self-deceptive sense of security. The film wreaks havoc with the traditional forms of perception that determine its ideologically bound view of the world. Renoir's breach of trust was evident in the unsympathetic reception the film received upon its release, and in the fact that it was unrecuperable to bourgeois cinema for twenty years, until its restoration in 1959. Of all Renoir's films, only *La Vie est à nous* had a longer underground existence.

While Renoir appears to prefer morality to politics as a subject, he is all the time exposing to his contemporaries just how politicized their morality actually is. As complicated as the plot of *La Règle du jeu* may be, its indebtedness to classical comic conventions and rules of construction is so obviously foregrounded as to compel the audience's notice. I have mentioned that Renoir's first synopsis for his film was a modernised adaptation of Alfred de Musset's *Les Caprices de Marianne* (1833). Additional formative influences were Marivaux's *Le Jeu de l'amour et du hasard* (1730) and Beaumarchais's *Le Mariage de Figaro* (1784), a play which is to the French Revolution as *La Règle du jeu* is to the Second World War. Renoir recalled that he listened to French baroque music, to Couperin, Rameau, "and every composer from Lulli to Grétry," which gave him a "wish to film the sort of people who danced to that music."[41] If this music is not actually to be heard in the finished film, it is nevertheless there by association. Robert's mechanical musical toys perfectly epitomize him as a charming, trivial creature of the eighteenth century and its obsession with a clockwork universe of order and regularity. He is the proper if somewhat vulgar descendant of that bourgeoisie for whom Renoir's dramatic and musical sources

[41] Renoir, *My Life and My Films*, p. 169.

wrote. But those cultural models were the product of a particular way of seeing, which in turn produced a particular social reality. That social reality had changed, however, so to play—as Renoir does—with the forms of perception that mediated one's lived experience of that earlier reality in this period of crisis is to expose the anachronism of its values. More profoundly, one should note the irony of drawing upon classical French comedy for a film that represents the class which produced and lived this rich cultural heritage as morally bankrupt and politically reactionary. The social formation that is scrutinized by drawing upon the cultural resources of that tradition will preserve its privileges at any hypocritical cost. The man of the modern age, the man of this new mechanical age of risk and speed, André Jurieu, threatens to disrupt by his sincere importunities both the formal structure of this classical comedy as well as the smug security of the class that it symbolizes. That "deplorable accident," the shooting of André Jurieu, forestalls the possibility of a continuously open-ended narrative (with love triangles perpetuated ad infinitum), preserves the formal closure necessitated by the preordained comic structure, in other words, and at the same time enables the social world represented in the film to close its ranks once again. No change can be permitted, no threat endured. *La Règle du jeu* deploys a form that is the perfect containment of society's moral and political intransigence and a register of the film's pessimism at the possibilities for social change.

In my discussion of *Le Crime de M. Lange* I mentioned that a murder is the pivotal action in many of Renoir's films of the thirties. In that film and in the other films prior to *La Règle du jeu* the murderer is forced outside the prevailing social formation because his action is a threat to society as it is presently constituted. The threat comes from the challenge that he offers, in the name of justice, moral or political, to oppressive social forces. But here, for the first time, the murderer (Schumacher, played by Gaston Modot) acts on behalf of society, is accepted back into society *because* he has committed this act, and his act is justified by society's spokesman, Robert. Once it is described as an "accident," no one has to accept responsibility and no self-knowledge has to be admitted. In the earlier films murder is an act of rebellion—the most serious social crime next to collective revolution—committed by a solitary protagonist, and frequently committed on behalf of some alternative social interests as well as his own. *La Règle du jeu*, on the other hand, has no individual protagonist—certainly not Schumacher—so in a very real sense its murder is committed by the prevailing social formation, although it is not the less a political murder for that. In one sense, of course, shooting André Jurieu can be regarded as a *crime passionel*, as can the murders of Lulu, Albert, and Batala. Schumacher's injured feelings have driven him to revenge. But Schumacher's feelings have been produced in a society in which personal attachments are invariably weaker than social bonds or social codes. Fidelity is no more than an appearance, and love is but "the exchange of two fantasies and the contact of two skins."[42]

Those earlier films that anticipate social change *do* envisage a society in which there is room for private feelings and personal intimacy (Toni and Josefa, Lange and Valentine, Pepel and Natasha, Maréchal and Elsa). Here, however, Lisette prefers the benefits of service with "Madame" to a relationship with her husband. Ironically, Schumacher is not aware, until the deed is done, that he is acting on behalf of society. Mistaking Christine for Lisette and André for Octave, he is at the mercy of a "plot"— the preordained comic form, the rules of the game of love in society—which will absorb his private revolt. And by not shooting either Octave or Christine, but André Jurieu, he unwittingly

---

[42] Geneviève makes the remark in the film, quoting, as she says, Nicolas-Sébastien Roch Chamfort's precept to the effect that "l'amour dans la société, c'est l'échange de deux fantaisies et le contact de deux épidermes." See the definitive screenplay of *La Règle du jeu* in *L'Avant-Scène du Cinéma*, no. 52 (October 1965), p. 19.

preserves the status quo. He gets rid of an interloper, who in breaking the rules of the game, inadvertently threatens to expose the insecurity and moral confusion of a decadent society. Finally, he has not resolved his relationship with his wife at all. Schumacher is the dupe of forces that subjugate his personal feelings. There is no room in this society for private revolt or personal motive. The rules will encompass everyone. Those whom they cannot encompass will be shot (André) or expelled (Marceau, Octave). The power (and hypocrisy) of the social codes is well illustrated by the meaning of Schumacher's momentary expulsion from Robert's service. He is let go, because, as a gamekeeper, he has claimed extraterritorial privileges in hunting Marceau about the château. He has got on the wrong costume for that pursuit in this setting. Were he actually to shoot Marceau in the château he would be no better than a cold-blooded murderer. His domain is the outdoors. So when he shoots André Jurieu in the garden of La Colinière he is in his element, performing his rightful duty, which permits Robert's justification that Schumacher fired because he thought he saw a poacher. André dies like one of those rabbits brutally slaughtered during the hunt. Finally, *La Règle du jeu* puts the seal on that omnipresent conflict in Renoir's films of the thirties between the differing claims of justice and the law since it permits no distinction to be made. There may be no justice in the description of André Jurieu's death as a "deplorable accident," but the law will accept the excuse since society acted in defense of its own interests.

What irony is to be found in the fact that Schumacher, of Germanic origin, commits the violence that society accepts as justifiable in the name of peace and its collective security? There can be no doubt that the aristocrats and the *haute bourgeoisie* represent for Renoir the class interests that betrayed the Popular Front, outlawed Republican Spain, and consented to Munich. But in a way, the world of *La Règle du jeu* is bleaker still. While the preceding films of the thirties did not literally re-present any *existing* historical reality of the period, they intimated what they would like that reality to be by recognizing the end of the ruling class (*Le Crime de M. Lange, La Vie est à nous, La Grande Illusion, La Marseillaise*), or by allowing its "unity" with the working class (*Les Bas-Fonds*). However, the disillusionment of *La Règle du jeu* is such that the ruling class seems permanently ensconced and class conflict, or class consciousness, never raises its head. The servants are but the apes of their masters, in their fads, their fashions, and their gossip, and even act on behalf of their masters to preserve the structure of society as it is.

What, then, is the plight of the committed artist-intellectual in this situation? However fortuitous the casting of Renoir in the part of Octave may have been in fact, we cannot deny that the merging of the man with the role encourages us to see the director of the film as speaking both "in" and "out" of character. The allusive license brought about by the casting produces a rupture within the film's process of signification, a tension between its signifying practice and the extratextual social reality to which it provides access, thereby opening up a place for the spectator to compare his critical judgement on the world in which he lives with that uttered by the film. At those moments when Renoir speaks out of the character of Octave, we cannot avoid the recognition that *La Règle du jeu* refers to the world outside itself virtually in the form of direct address:

> If I didn't have a few friends who support me ... well, I would die of hunger. And yet, you know, when I was young I too thought that I would have something to say for myself. Contact with the public, you see ... that's the thing I would have liked to experience. That, that must be ... it must be shattering, eh? When I think that it's passed me by ... well, it does something to me. Then I try to ... to rack my brains, to work out what happened. Except to reach that point I have to have had a little drink. You

know, back there, on the steps, just now, I thought that it had actually happened. Oh dear! Only, after that, well . . . one goes from bad to worse . . . so a bad moment has to be lived through. One gets used to it, huh? Oh dear! What a beautiful night, eh! Here, look at the moon, look at it.[43]

Octave's frustration and despair, even the self-denigrating conception of his character, are perhaps a product of Renoir's sense of his failure to influence audiences on behalf of Popular Front interests, despite the commercial popularity of many of his films. The psychology of Octave's character in the film is perhaps a function of Renoir's legitimate social disillusionment. Renoir himself has said that Octave is "the confidant of all the others, the hero in spite of himself."[44] Octave can be the confidant of all the other characters because his position as an artist grants him social mobility. He is equally at home (or not at home, as the case may be) with both masters and servants, upper class and lower, flirting with Lisette, familiar with Christine. As a *failed* artist, however, he is now a sponger, a parasite, a court jester whose good-natured buffoonery pays his keep. And to further the denigration of Octave, it is as well to remember that in traditional comedy his role is that of the pander. There are important vestiges of that role here, for it is he who sets the love game, the plot, in motion by introducing André Jurieu to La Colinière. Like the conventional pander, he is impotent. Too old to run away with Christine, depressed in spirit, poor in purse, he sends André Jurieu in his stead. In doing so he brings the love game to a halt. (He is the *metteur-en-scène* of this bizarre "plot"!) Is there not evidence of despair in the fact that it is the artist-intellectual who sends the one sincere (if clumsy) man in

[43] Jean Renoir, *Rules of the Game*, trans. John McGrath and Maureen Teitelbaum (New York: Simon and Schuster, 1970), p. 157.

[44] This was said in an interview with Marguerite Bussot on 28 June 1939, and reprinted in *Premier Plan*, nos. 22-23-24 (May 1962), p. 278.

this society to his death, thereby confirming the ineluctable power of the rules of the game? (Parenthetically, the film's pessimistic reading of history is complete when one remarks that the potentially disruptive André Jurieu—our incipient protagonist—is himself an object of satire in his clumsiness and judged not to be worth saving because too ineffectual.) As the hero in spite of himself, Octave is the antihero: it is by inadvertence that he reveals the ruthless, hypocritical nature of this society *to us*, for he does not know when he gives André his coat that Schumacher waits by the little greenhouse with a loaded gun. As an artist-intellectual Octave no longer has a purposeful, instructive role to play *in this society*. Appropriately, while the comic plot and the relationships between the characters spin out of control during the fête and its aftermath, Octave is helplessly imprisoned in his bear costume.

In acknowledgement of his failure (and even his cowardice), Octave banishes himself at the film's end. Consistent with his characterization in the film, it is Octave's position as court jester that gives him the license to make certain perceptive observations about the world with impunity:

Octave: I feel like . . . like disappearing down a hole.
Robert: And what would that achieve for you?
Octave: Well, it would help me not to see anything anymore, not to search anymore, for what's good, and what's bad. Because, you see, on this earth, there is one thing which is terrible, and that is that everyone has their own good reasons.
Robert: But, of course, everyone has their own good reasons—and I, I want everyone to give them freely. I am against barriers, you know, I am against walls. Anyway, that's why I'm going to invite André.[45]

---

[45] Renoir, *Rules of the Game*, p. 53.

Octave: We're in a period when everyone tells lies: phar-
macists' handbills, governments, the radio, the cinema,
the newspapers. . . . So how could you expect us poor
individuals not to lie as well?[46]

These latter remarks concerning the universality of lying in
contemporary society, along with the frozen moment in which
Octave attempts to conduct the imaginary orchestra, as well as
the passage previously quoted in which he confesses that he is
a parasite and bemoans his failure to make contact with a public,
were all cut from the film prior to its release in the shortened
97 minute version. Perhaps the distributor simply anticipated
the censor's objection to the allusiveness of these comments. The
remarks above are certainly not an instance of Octave's (or
Renoir's) moral confusion. Octave is unambiguously open-eyed.
To defend "everyone has their own good reasons"—as Robert
does—is to defend the fact that "everyone tells lies." Octave does
not willingly do that. If there is a "reason" to justify every action,
then "good" and "bad" become hopelessly relative, and the need
to accept any responsibility is avoided. The moral confusion is
Robert's, for his response to Octave is consistent with his remark
to Schumacher that he does not want fences and he does not
want rabbits either. The ultimate consequence is the death of
André Jurieu, excused with an appropriate "reason." Octave's
problem is that he can perceive the situation that has given rise
to the state of affairs he describes, but he can no longer *do*
anything about it. The bleak finality of *La Règle du jeu* as a
judgement on the disintegration of French society in 1939 and
the moral/political role of the artist-intellectual makes Renoir's
self-exile almost inevitable.

Whatever contemporary reviewers may have thought of the
film[47]—and generally they thought very little of it, failing to

[46] Ibid., p. 155.
[47] For an anthology of generous excerpts from contemporary reviews, see *"La Règle*

119

understand its formal daring, catch the point of its shifting moods, or grasp fully the object of its bitter satire—*La Règle du jeu* knows itself as the product of a political crisis. For the moment, Renoir himself was still marginally active on behalf of the Parti Communiste Français. In February 1939 he helped found and direct the Office de Documentation Cinématographique for the purpose of bringing to public attention films that received no exhibition for either commercial or censorship reasons. The office was described by one journalist as "cette boutique d'images staliniennes."[48] Along with Louis Aragon and Léon Moussinac, both Communists, Renoir was a patron of a major exhibition of nineteenth-century French photography. And as president of the ciné-club of Ciné-liberté he organised a February evening devoted to the work of Marcel Pagnol. On 8 July, the day after the première of *La Règle du jeu*, Renoir was to have introduced Joris Ivens's *400 Millions* to a benefit for Les Amis du Peuple Chinois. Coincidentally, on the same day, 8 July, an interview with Renoir appeared in *Ce Soir* which reported that the next two or three film projects he had in mind would be shot in North Africa.[49] One surmises, therefore, although the evidence is not explicit, that from the end of 1938 through the first half of 1939 Renoir's alliance with the PCF gradually deteriorated. Certainly he had made up his mind to leave France before the disastrous reception of *La Règle du jeu*; and certainly we are entitled to see *La Règle du jeu* in the aspect of a manifesto. However, it was not to North Africa that Renoir went, but to Italy, to make *La Tosca* with Carl Koch and Luchino Visconti, much to the chagrin of the PCF and Louis Aragon, who wrote in *Ce Soir* for 12 August:

---

du jeu et la critique en 1939," ed. Claude Gauteur, *Image et Son*, no. 282 (March 1974), pp. 49-73.

[48] Ibid., p. 58.

[49] Ibid., p. 53.

I also write this for you personally, Jean Renoir, who have left Paris without bidding me goodbye ... for those who are weak or cowardly ... for those who have too soon despaired of France, and who, perhaps, I shall no longer be able to regard calmly after this film, and this war, and this great Passion of the people of Spain, my brother.[50]

What seemed to the Communists like running away from France in her hour of need, or even implicit collaboration with a fascist power—for such were their accusations—received some measure of vindication on 23 August when Nazi Germany and the Soviet Union signed a nonaggression pact. Stalin had made his own bargain with Hitler, and the Parti Communiste Français was exposed to the barbs of the Right as no better (if not worse) than the government it righteously professed to criticize. The credibility of the Party plummeted immediately, and left-wing fellow travellers hastily withdrew their last shred of support. The isolated Party faithful had now to perform an about-face, abandon their patriotic stand, and defend the Nazi-Soviet pact. Now regarded as a threat to national security, the Party was dissolved by the government and its publications suspended on 26 September 1939. Whatever may have been Renoir's particular thoughts at this time, one supposes that his general disillusionment was complete. With *La Tosca*—Renoir arrived in Rome on 14 July to begin work—Renoir had effectively begun his second, nonpolitical career as a film maker. But he was not passive, and he did *not* abandon his patriotism. When France went to war with Germany on 3 September, Renoir returned to Paris and entered the Service Cinématographique de l'Armée as a lieutenant. Renoir was now forty-five years of age. During

---

[50] *Image et Son*, no. 268 (February 1973), p. 11. "This film" is André Malraux's *L'Espoir* and "this war" the Spanish Civil War. *L'Espoir* was given a private screening to a select audience in Paris in July 1939. This screening must have been the occasion for Aragon's praise. The film had no public release until after the war.

the long months of the "phoney war" he apparently worked on some propaganda material until he was advised by the Ministère des Informations in the spring of 1940 to return to Italy and take up *La Tosca* again in support of diplomatic manoeuvres aimed at securing Italy's continued neutrality. With the declaration of war by Italy on 10 June 1940, and *La Tosca* uncompleted, Renoir returned to France and joined the exodus of refugees headed south away from the advancing German troops. Whether Renoir had reason to fear for his life or his liberty under Vichy, in view of the increasing number of trials and oppressive measures taken against Communists and their sympathizers, I do not know. Certainly Renoir's departure for the United States, negotiated with the help of Robert Flaherty, was only a matter of time after July 1940. After the frustration of considerable delay, he finally emigrated in December 1940, and arrived in New York on New Year's Eve.

CHAPTER THREE

INTERREGNUM:
THIS LAND IS MINE, THE SOUTHERNER

Something very important happened to me along with millions of other people, and this was the Second World War, which had been the cause of my departure for America where I met some very important people for me, and where it seemed to me that I was born a second time.

JEAN RENOIR, 1952

In six-and-one-half years Renoir made five feature films in Hollywood (and one documentary in New York for the Office of War Information, *Salute to France*, 1944), and worked for three different studios (Fox, Universal, RKO), as well as producing independently. Renoir's attitude towards Hollywood, like his attitude towards America, has always been ambivalent. On the one hand he was grateful for the opportunity to make films, on the other he was dissatisfied and ill at ease with the prevailing system of production:

Without regretting my first American films, I know for sure that they represent nothing of my ideal. . . .

America remains the only country in the world where any director, provided his name is not completely unknown, can borrow the money necessary to shoot a film as he wants.[1]

On account of the exceedingly high cost of film-making, the studios cannot risk their money without what they call security. Security consists of the script, the work-plan: and

---

[1] From an essay first published in 1948, and reprinted in Jean Renoir, *Ecrits 1926-1971*, ed. Claude Gauteur (Paris: Belfond, 1974), pp. 54, 57-58.

every detail must be fixed beforehand by a sort of administrative council, consisting of the studio chiefs, producer and director. If a director can talk well, he can usually get his own way so long as he forecasts precisely what that will be. This is something I cannot do. . . . In other words, what has been said of the tyranny of the large studios is sometimes true, but it depends upon individuals. Personally, I should have worked there without being in the least bit tyrannised, in fact most amiably, if I had the gift of foreseeing just what I wanted to do on the floor. But I haven't.[2]

A full account of Renoir's Hollywood years would have to reckon with this ambivalence, for he was never more unsure of himself than during these six and a half years.[3]

On the personal level, Renoir's emigration to the United States in his middle age was the beginning of a long exile from "le sol qui le nourrit," which he spent trying to reconcile a life divided between one country and another. He never again seemed at home in either country: he took out dual citizenship, maintained two residences, and worked at mastering two languages. One country was forever lost, the other forever alien: he came to regard France and the past with nostalgia, while he accepted America and the present resolutely:

We forget that while in a foreign land we try to re-live the country of our childhood, the shape of that country is constantly changing. And with it the spirit changes. We return after a few years to the scenes of our youth and find that we cannot recognize them. That is why, for our peace

[2] From an interview with Jacques Rivette and François Truffaut, published in English as "Renoir in America," *Sight and Sound* 24, no. 3 (July-September 1954), p. 12.

[3] William Gilcher's doctoral dissertation, "Jean Renoir in America: A Critical Analysis of His Major Films from *Swamp Water* to *The River*" (The University of Iowa, 1979), offers the most detailed account of Renoir's years in the United States in relation to the production histories of the films he made there. The very recent publication of *Lettres d'Amérique*, edited by Dido Renoir and Alexander Sesonske (Paris: Presses de la Renaissances, 1984), will shed new light on Renoir's complex attitude towards America.

of mind, we must try to escape from the spell of memories. Our salvation lies in plunging resolutely into the hell of the new world, a world horizontally divided, a world without passion or nostalgia. We must forget the bistro in Magagnosc.[4]

Perhaps something of the professional frustration attending Renoir's American experience can be communicated by noting his unrealised projects. On separate occasions he had wanted to film *Wind, Sand, and Stars* and *Night Flight*, both by Antoine de Saint-Exupéry, whom Renoir had met during his trans-Atlantic voyage to the United States and who resided with the Renoirs in Hollywood for a time. Based on his own experience as a refugee from Paris to Cagnes-sur-Mer in June and July 1940, as the German occupying troops advanced deep into France, Renoir wanted to make a film about the exodus of children from Paris to the Midi. René Clément dealt with the subject in his *Jeux interdits* of 1952. The *New York Times* announced two abortive Renoir projects in 1941. On 14 April it was stated that he would direct *The Night the World Shook* from a screenplay by Nunnally Johnson, and on 3 May he was about to direct Dwight Taylor's adaptation of Stephen Fisher's novel *I Wake Up Screaming* (eventually shot by Bruce Humberstone). Renoir's ill-fated connection with Universal Studios lasted three days in 1942, when he began a production of *The Amazing Mrs. Holliday* with Deanna Durbin (completed by Bruce Manning). At some point he evidently expressed an interest in following Orson Welles to South America (*It's All True*, 1942) and doing some filming for the United States government war effort. In 1944 Renoir travelled to Minnesota to meet Sister Elizabeth Kenny, but Dudley Nichols produced and directed the film *Sister Kenny*. The next failure was a Renoir–Nichols adaptation of Mary Webb's *Precious Bane* with Ingrid Bergman. No financial backer could be found who would accept Bergman in the role of a woman with a harelip.

[4] Jean Renoir, *My Life and My Films* (New York: Atheneum, 1974), pp. 281-282.

Montgomery Clift was in mind for a Renoir–Nichols remake of
Les Bas-Fonds in a Los Angeles setting. James Mason's contract
with Walter Wanger for *The Reckless Moment* gave him directorial approval. He approved of Jean Renoir; Renoir accepted
the assignment; but for reasons undiscovered Max Ophuls directed the film. And finally, one other lost project during this
period was an adaptation of Clifford Odets's *Night Music* with
Dana Andrews and Joan Bennett, to be produced by the Film
Group, an independent production company that Renoir had
founded with Burgess Meredith.

Of course there are a multitude of unrealised projects in every
film maker's career. But in Renoir's case he seems to have done
a good deal of casting about in the United States in the forties
as he looked at projects that were variously French, American,
British, or German, original projects and adaptations, and with
no consistent collaborator (David Flaherty at one point, Charles
David at another, then Nichols, Charles Laughton, Odets, Frank
Ryan, and Meredith). It is impossible to discover a direction in
all this fruitless searching about, or for that matter in the films
that Renoir did complete. I think Renoir's sojourn in Hollywood
must be regarded as a second apprenticeship—the first being his
silent-film work in France in the twenties—an interregnum, a
period of reappraisal that would eventually bear fruit with the
maturity of his second career in the fifties. In view of the great
shift in style and theme that is manifest in the work of the fifties,
this long period of reappraisal was doubtless necessary after the
disillusionment with *La Règle du jeu*, the betrayal of his political
aspirations, and his forced exile from France.

The difficulties of adaptation, both personal and professional,
produced an uneven body of work in America: banal (*Swamp
Water*, 1941), rhetorical (*This Land Is Mine*, 1943), maudlin (*The
Southerner*, 1945), frivolous (*The Diary of a Chambermaid*, 1946),
and incomplete (*The Woman On the Beach*, 1947). If Renoir's
entire career consisted solely of these productions, his work
would have been forgotten. It is generally accepted that not one

of Renoir's American films is entirely satisfactory. Their critical defense has been based on stylistic or thematic links with various of the French films, as part of the effort to preserve the wholeness of an *oeuvre* and the notion of a unified authorial consciousness. But these films have not much in common even with one another, as though Renoir had not yet found his way after the loss of France, and without a familiar cast or crew. He takes his material from novels or short stories (sometimes English, sometimes French), shoots now in the studio and now on location, at the mercy of studio styles, different generic categories, and the exigencies of a different marketplace. In short, these films are the work of a man who does not seem sure where he is going. To group them according to some common style or common theme seems futile. Two films, however, do give us a clue to where Renoir might be going. I want to examine *This Land Is Mine* because I think its latent text is a reevaluation of the immediate past; while the visual strategies and thematic emphases of *The Southerner* seem to me to anticipate the future. I do not argue that there is continuity between the French thirties, the American forties, and the European fifties—not at all; there is instead an epistemological and ideological rupture that these two films may help us understand. This rupture will mean a radical change for the social function of art and the role of the artist-intellectual.

"Somewhere in Europe," a title informs us, a town is newly occupied by advancing German forces. Albert Lory (Charles Laughton) is a timid schoolteacher of uncertain age who lives with his self-indulgent and possessive mother (Una O'Connor). Demonstrating little in the way of moral or political resistance and nothing in the way of physical resistance, Lory offers a servile welcome to the invader by destroying his copy of the clandestine resistance newspaper and by censoring his schoolbooks. Terrified of violence, Lory exposes his cowardice to his students and his colleagues, among whom are the beautiful Louise Martin (Maureen O'Hara), who looks upon the invader with fiery contempt. Louise's fiancé, George Lambert (George

Sanders), is a willing collaborationist who accepts the arguments of the German commandant Major von Keller (Walter Slezak) that the "new order" will bring about the political, economic, and moral regeneration of Europe. When George rationalizes his acquiescence in the German occupation to Louise, she breaks their engagement. Meanwhile, her brother, Paul (Kent Smith), is an active member of the resistance movement and manages to sabotage a supply train. The school's headmaster, Professor Sorel (Philip Merivale), is responsible for publishing the resistance newspaper. Following the assassination of two German soldiers and the destruction of an ammunition train, Major von Keller is obliged to take hostages (among them Albert Lory and Professor Sorel). To bring about the release of her son, Mrs. Lory tells George that she suspects Paul of responsibility for the acts of sabotage. George promptly tells the authorities. Paul is killed, whereupon George commits suicide in a fit of remorse. Discovered at the scene of the suicide, Lory is accused of George's murder but seems likely to be freed when he manages to persuade Major von Keller of his innocence. However, while Lory is awaiting the resumption of his trial he witnesses the execution of Professor Sorel and must thereupon acknowledge the truth of Nazi tyranny. In a long, abstract address to the court Lory denounces both German oppression and the moral corruption of collaboration. Found not guilty of murder, he is admired by Louise for overcoming his cowardice and speaking the truth in defense of freedom. Now a hero, Lory is arrested by the Germans in his classroom the next day while reading to his students the Declaration of the Rights of Man. There can be no mistaking the didacticism of the conclusion, which has been brought about by a melodramatic concatentation of incidents.

Of all Renoir's American features, only *This Land Is Mine* was made from an original treatment (written with Dudley Nichols). And at RKO Charles Koerner gave Renoir and Nichols complete freedom to do as they wished. In taking the Occupation as his subject Renoir chose an immediate historical event of

personal concern and evidently approached it with the same
conviction he brought to the causes he espoused in his French
films of the thirties: "Jean Renoir had lately come from Europe
and was a volcano of feeling as a result of what he had seen
and experienced."[5] If Dudley Nichols is to be believed, Renoir
invested more of his personal energies and private feelings in
this project than in any other of his American films. Why, then,
did it turn out awry? To explain the film's brutal reception by
the French press when it was shown in Paris as Renoir's first
American feature to reach there after the war, Renoir claimed
that it was made for American audiences who had been led by
propaganda to assume that France was a country of collaborationists. Renoir says that he wanted to show that daily life in
an occupied country is not so easy as people are led to believe,
that the conditions for action and response are by no means
unambiguous. One can appreciate why the postwar French
might find the film's recipe for heroism so much vacuous idealism, and the film's protagonist either too passive or, at the
worst, an instance of Renoir's own intellectual vanity, easily
secured by the enabling distance of the Atlantic Ocean. (In some
quarters the film fueled lingering accusations that Renoir had
completely lost touch with his origins.)[6] Whatever Renoir's intent
may have been, the film is so openly rhetorical as thoroughly to

[5] Dudley Nichols, "The Writer and the Film," in *Twenty Best Film Plays*, ed. John
Gassner and Dudley Nichols (New York: Crown, 1943), p. xxxviii.

[6] The editors of *Premier Plan*, nos. 22-23-24 (May 1962), p. 302, observe that *This Land
Is Mine* had scarcely a critical admirer, other than the collaborator Maurice Bardèche!
They also reprint a contemporary review by Joseph Prudhomme, which reads in part:
"I am certain that if M. Renoir—in another time and another place once a film maker
of quality—had lived in Paris or in any one of our provincial cities when the German
troops practiced their 'good manners' he would not have dared to commit so many
flagrant inaccuracies. ... He would not even have dared to make this film. ... It is
possible that when he conceived *This Land Is Mine* he was full of good intentions. In
our eyes good intentions do not excuse bad cinema and we regret that a Frenchman
has, even unintentionally, given a ridiculously distorted image of the suffering and
courage through which so many Frenchmen bought the right to be proud at the cost
of so many lives (pp. 305-306)."

dilute its conviction. In this respect, Dudley Nichols's admission that the film "seemed like a morality play" is much to the point but not to the advantage of the film.[7] Perhaps it is the very dilution of this conviction that makes *This Land Is Mine* the most problematic film of Renoir's entire career.

I believe that, through Albert Lory, the film inadvertently expresses a will to believe in the possibility of the assumption of influence and authority—of heroism even—on the part of an otherwise passive figure. What I am trying to suggest is that the more closely one looks at *This Land Is Mine* the less it appears to be a tale about the general difficulties of life in an occupied country, treated at arm's length for the illumination of American audiences, and the more it appears to wrestle with an artistic (and moral) crisis of the very first importance. This crisis is apparent from the formal strategies of the text, from the characterisations and the narrative, not from the choice of subject per se. Peter Harcourt, to whom I am indebted for the hint, is alone among critics in having recognized the possibility of such a crisis:

> ... *This Land Is Mine* might seem to be one of the most directly personal, even the most confessional film that Renoir ever made. It is stiff and stilted in many of its details (as his films in English frequently are); but it contains within it a magnificent performance by Charles Laughton and it very much conveys the need to take up a position when faced with the war, to lose one's hesitations and take a stand. Just how this film might relate to Renoir's own life, it would be difficult to say (and not really necessary).[8]

While I cannot agree with Harcourt on all points (Laughton's performance is something less than "magnificent," and I am not persuaded that hesitations are honestly lost), I believe that this

[7] Nichols, "The Writer and the Film," p. xxxix.

[8] Peter Harcourt, *Six European Directors* (Harmondsworth: Penguin Books, 1974), pp. 80-81.

is indeed a strongly autobiographical film. It is remarkable, therefore, that *This Land Is Mine* should nearly follow upon the equally autobiographical *La Règle du jeu*: only the incomplete *La Tosca* and the uninteresting *Swamp Water* come between them. As I will show, the two films do touch each other in more than a fugitive way. But I use the word "autobiographical" carelessly, for I do not mean to suppose that either of these films is intended as autobiography. And I do not wish to read the man in and through the work by constructing a subjective personality outside the text. The text remains the site of meaning, not some anterior consciousness of the artist. What I do mean is that *This Land Is Mine* is a rephrasing of the conflict that led to and beyond *La Règle du jeu*, a conflict determined historically, and constructed, like Renoir himself, out of the contradictory ideological positions of a decade of political strife. Whereas *La Règle du jeu* is the brilliant summation of the artist-intellectual's experience of the thirties, *This Land Is Mine* gropes with the consequences of Octave's self-exile. One speculates that *This Land Is Mine* raises questions about the responsibilities of the artist following Renoir's departure from France in her moment of humiliation and defeat. If there is something to this speculation, I do not think Renoir's inability to resolve the problem at this time has anything at all to do with either his ignorance or his knowledge of life in an occupied country. The informational documentary *Salute to France*, made for the Office of War Information in 1944 more or less anonymously, is proof that Renoir could articulate the cost of collaboration. But then, as a "document" that film is a great deal less problematic than *This Land Is Mine*.

One might begin to investigate the latent text of *This Land Is Mine* by looking at its portrait of Major von Keller—a brilliant conception of "how plausible and attractive Fascism can appear to some people."[9] As played by Walter Slezak, the character is

[9] Nichols, "The Writer and the Film," p. xxxix.

charming, urbane, even witty. He is one in a line of such characters from Renoir's films—Jules Berry's Batala, Erich von
Stroheim's Von Rauffenstein, Pierre Renoir's Louis XVI, Marcel
Dalio's Marquis—characters who do not seem so much like
villains as like scoundrels, although that judgement is a tribute
to the subtlety of their conception rather than their moral or
social identities. Major von Keller is, in a way, first cousin to
Robert, the Marquis de la Chesnaye of *La Règle du jeu*, even to
the antique music box with which he toys in a couple of scenes.
With their comfortable manners and their respect for tradition,
one feels the two of them would hit it off famously. They belong
to a dying breed; they both have style (or "class," as the General
of *La Règle du jeu* says). Another way to put it would be to say
that Robert, with his good-natured grace and seeming tolerance
("But, of course, everyone has their own good reasons—and I,
I want everyone to give them freely"), leads the way to a Major
von Keller, whose calculating intelligence can rationalize Robert's confusion and act for his indecision. Robert is the sort of
Frenchman, ultimately satirized in *La Règle du jeu* for his triviality and hypocrisy, who welcomed the Major von Kellers because they offered the restoration of "order" to a society whose
traditional structure was perilously near collapse. That is precisely what Von Keller offers to the collaborationists in *This
Land Is Mine*.

Von Keller is a success as an ideologue and a soldier because
he is convinced of his own position, and offers the same plausible
conviction to those who will listen. Of course, the "new order"
that Major von Keller will bring to Europe means moral corruption for all who accede to it, but it will not seem like that
to those less clever or more insecure than he. Historically, it will
also mean political hegemony, economic imperialism, racism,
and violence; but what is superior about the conception of Major
von Keller in *This Land Is Mine* is that the military force that
he represents is understated in favour of his ideological persua-
siveness. Major von Keller is not the swaggering, jack-booted
psychotic of impoverished literary or cinematic imaginations.

On the basis of Dudley Nichols's account, he and Renoir would seem to have known what they were up to:

> There was no villain in the drama. We had ruled him out at the outset, for there are no villains in life but only human beings embodying elements of good and evil. . . . For myself I must say that I discovered many truths about one modern aspect of good and evil by wrestling with the lives of these characters. I discovered how plausible and attractive Fascism can appear to some people, and if we do not face that truth we can never triumph over it. I saw how much of it there was around me, how much of it perhaps in my own heart. That too must be faced if we are to win over evil.[10]

It is the tyranny of the *ideology* of Nazism for which Major von Keller is the articulate spokesman, and that ideology is shown to be effective—and attractive—because it masquerades as a superior humanism. Major von Keller seems decent, tolerant of other points of view, rational, and apparently willing to support the values of humanity in the best sense. That is why he is conceived as a man of taste and learning who can quote Tacitus (in Latin), and is familiar with Plato, Juvenal, Voltaire, and Shakespeare ("We love him in Germany. The English don't understand him."). The portrait is wholly credible and deeply disturbing. For the historical reality is that there were European intellectuals of sound mind who were taken in by this masquerade, just as there are still people who think of themselves as well-informed and liberal ready to make concessions to various species of totalitarianism, whether in El Salvador, in Chile, or in South Africa.

Major von Keller's perversion of humanistic values has a nice logic. On the Occupation:

> We are both working for this war to be over. Only then can we have a peaceful and united Europe. And only then

[10] Ibid.

can your country—and men like you—regain their dignity and honour.[11]

On collaboration:

> Of course we Germans could take over courts, schools, town halls, the administration of the whole country—but we're not tyrants—we prefer not to do that. We prefer to collaborate, to give freedom to the nations we defeat on the battlefield. But freedom must be limited by the necessities of war. We're still fighting on other fronts. It's a very small sacrifice we ask of you, when we are still sacrificing our lives for the future happiness of the world. You see, I'm frank, I have nothing to conceal.[12]

On the taking of hostages:

> If we call it sabotage I shall have to take hostages from the town—and shoot them finally if the guilty are not found. I don't like to shoot innocent people and I don't like to make martyrs—once you begin that it never stops until finally we'll find ourselves sitting on a powderkeg. I've noticed what happens in our districts which we are protecting.[13]

There is no fanaticism here, only the beguiling subtlety of evil. By appealing to his audience in the name of dignity, honour, freedom, self-sacrifice, law and order—those noble values to which the Western mind responds like a physical reflex—Major von Keller demonstrates a firm intellectual grasp of the ethical appeal of the ideology of humanism in the Western tradition. Historically, people like him were formed by these values and assented to them.

One understands why reviewers like James Agate were dis-

---

[11] *This Land Is Mine*, in *Twenty Best Film Plays*, p. 847.
[12] Ibid., p. 869.
[13] Ibid., p. 846.

concerted by the portrait of Major von Keller because of what
was taken to be an unconscious sympathy for his kind on the
part of the film makers: "Let me repeat that I distrust that
portraiture which shows the Nazi as a man in whose mouth
butter has not even a tendency to melt."[14] But what a hell of
uncertainty is opened up by such a portrait! Agate is wrong to
imply that Renoir is of the devil's party without knowing it.
Renoir *understands* Major von Keller. No doubt he knew such
people in France in the late thirties, or at least knew people with
the same twist of mind, inasmuch as *La Règle du jeu* foretells
the possibility of their willing collaboration with Nazism. There
is certainly one exchange in *This Land Is Mine* that is a direct
recollection of Renoir's own experience. George Lambert is con-
curring with Major von Keller about the social upheaval caused
by the working-class movement:

> *George*: Your ideas are exactly my ideas. I saw how our
> country was destroyed. False democratic ideas—women
> refusing to have children—strikes in all our factories for
> a 40 hour week while your people were working 70 and
> 80 hours a week. I want the new order for my country.
> I work for it. But I know we can't have it till this war
> is over. I must tell you the truth—I don't like the
> Occupation.[15]

Renoir might be alluding to his own commitment to causes of
the Popular Front (working class and antifascist), which were
betrayed by the class interests of the bourgeoisie and the aristocracy. The defeat of those causes led directly to the savage
pessimism of *La Règle du jeu* and indirectly to Renoir's departure

[14] James Agate, *Around Cinemas* (London: Home and Von Thal, 1946), p. 246.
[15] *This Land Is Mine*, p. 847. The "new order" promised by the Occupation, which
is invoked by George here and by Von Keller elsewhere in the film, may well be a
deliberate allusion to Marshal Pétain's famous collaborationist speech of 11 October 1940,
hailing Vichy as the start of a "new order" for France after the dissolution of the Third
Republic.

from France. It is worth noting that Major von Keller, with his *politesse* and his classical education, and George, with his managerial interests, are opposed by Paul Martin, who is evidently of the working class. Precisely that antagonism existed during the French thirties. Unfortunately, apart from the allusions I have cited, in *This Land Is Mine* the characters are not given a sufficiently specific social definition to draw out that antagonism along class lines.

In terms of the film's lack of social specificity, one has to agree with the frequent critical complaints of Renoir's factitious representation of a French provincial town in *This Land Is Mine*. The glaring antinaturalism of the studio sets might be seen as part of Renoir's movement away from the exterior realism of his location work in the thirties towards the interior realism (so-called) of his later years. But in his later work, when Renoir does promote the artifices of studio film-making, they are inseparable from his thematic concerns. He has not the least interest in the psychology of character or in being socially specific. One must, I think, attribute the failure to evoke a specific social milieu to the futility of attempting this within the Hollywood studio system. In the same vein, if I have not much to say about the visual style of *This Land Is Mine*, that is because it is utterly conventional (not to say uninspired). The framing, the compositions, the camera movements (such as they are), do nothing to socialize space, as in the manner of *Toni*, say, where we must understand that individual consciousness and class definition are integrated with the environment, so that the one determines the other. In *This Land Is Mine* the characters are not so much integrated *with* an environment as photographed *against* settings, so that their dimensionality is reduced in the artificiality of this space. Since we either ignore the sets altogether or simply refuse to grant them any credibility, the pretended social milieu lends almost nothing to the political or moral definition of the characters.

The specificity attributed to Major von Keller has been deduced from Walter Slezak's performance, allusion to other films directed by Renoir, presumptions about historical determinants, and reliance upon dialogue. The resort to dialogue is especially unfortunate, because it points to a basic weakness in the film. However brilliant the *conception* of Major von Keller may be, the *presentation* is unsatisfactory since its force depends almost entirely upon speech and performance rather than upon the mise-en-scène or the narrative. What Major von Keller represents is not challenged by the central narrative conflict of the film. There is not one interesting character on the French side who, throughout the duration of the narrative, has to grapple with the ideology for which Von Keller speaks. The conception of Major von Keller exists in a vacuum. What this means is that Major von Keller is but the nominal (and only the nominal) antagonist of the film, for the real conflict in the film does not lie with him, it lies elsewhere. Clearly it lies with Albert Lory, or I should say *within* Albert Lory. If Major von Keller is defined more or less historically, then Albert Lory is defined psychologically, and the two definitions are unassimilable. There is no evident connection between Lory's individual drama and the public drama of the German occupation for which Major von Keller is the mouthpiece. What interests Renoir in this film is not Major von Keller but the character of Albert Lory. By privileging Lory's psychological-emotional state, Renoir disturbs the *avowed* focus of his film and creates a serious narrative dislocation. And, as we shall see, when Renoir attempts to restore stability to his narrative at the film's conclusion, he plainly does not succeed.

What is the nature of Lory's individual drama? I take the essential aspect of Lory's character to be his cowardice, even as self-confessed in his next-to-last courtroom scene. But the *efficient cause* of Lory's cowardice is not, as one would suppose, the German presence in the occupied town. Lory's dependence on his mother—the absence of a husband/father is striking—is the heart of the matter in producing this character trait. After establishing a European, vaguely French wartime setting in the first scene, the second scene of the film is the domestic one between Lory and his mother, and despite discovery of the resistance newspaper and talk of the occupation, emphasis is upon this passive and unmanly son and his possessive, self-involved mother—an emphasis, in other words, upon idiosyncracies of character and character relationships. Certainly the salient details of the scene look to this emphasis: the surprising bottle of milk; Mrs. Lory's attention to Albert's appearance; her complaint about Louise's cat; the exaggeration of her rheumatism to win sympathy. In effect, the mother has castrated Lory with her suffocating demands for affection and obedience, thereby retarding his moral *and* sexual development. Hence Lory's undirected fear, cowardice, timidity. The presence of the German forces simply provides an occasion for the testing of this moral condition. Lory is then like an overgrown child in a world that expects him to behave with adult responsibility. Consistent with this characterisation is his lack of authority in the classroom scenes, scenes reminiscent both visually—the camera setups from the back of the room—and situationally—the unruly students, the chalkboard cartoon—of the representation of Professor Rath's inadequacy in *The Blue Angel*. But of paramount importance in relating Lory's timidity to his unmanliness is his adolescent infatuation with Louise Martin, of which Mrs. Lory is profoundly jealous, and of which Paul Martin makes a public jest.

Paul is the saboteur, and his active role in the film is shown to be consonant with sexual maturity. His relationship with his girlfriend appears to have no function in the film other than to establish his manliness. I do not mean that manliness is a requisite of heroism, and I do not suppose that Renoir and Nichols mean that it is, despite the clichés at work here. But in the film the equation seems to be made for the sake of defining Lory as a thoroughly passive and sexually alienated character. On reflection, therefore, the general social—or moral, or political—consequences of the German occupation are subordinated to Albert Lory's personal effort to break away from his mother by overcoming his cowardice and asserting his manhood. It is a matter of special note, then, that at the end of the film the mother should be ignored (and thus defeated) when Lory interrupts his courtroom speech on the need for resistance to declare publicly his love for Louise. In the court Mrs. Lory sits bowed between Louise on one side—who is shown in a couple of extreme closeups to be transfigured at Lory's words—and Paul's girlfriend on the other! We learn nothing of Mrs. Lory following the trial and Albert's release, but we do see Albert and Louise enter the school hand in hand, where he is to read the Declaration of the Rights of Man to his now well-behaved students prior to his final arrest. Lory has resolved the trauma of his cowardice, gained moral and political awareness, and reached sexual maturity all at once! Renoir has privileged an extraordinary character state through which to explore the difficulties of life in an occupied country. In fact, but for one brief encounter with Major von Keller in his prison cell, Lory is not shown to be attracted to fascism in the least. In his efforts to resolve his private dilemma, Lory's susceptibility is hardly at issue. And yet, given the avowed subject of the film and the fascinating portrait of Major von Keller, one might expect the film to concern itself with the invasion of Lory's consciousness by the ideology of Nazism. Instead, there is this serious disproportion between the film's public and private dramas. Why has the film displaced Lory's psychological-emotional state away from active encounter with Nazi ideology and into his relationship with his mother? That question cannot be answered directly, but the displacement of this character state does have implications for the artistic crisis exposed by the film.

I have said that when Renoir does attempt to stabilize his narrative by dovetailing the resolution of Lory's private drama with the resolution of the public drama of the consequences of the German occupation it does not work. It does not work because it is forced by a kind of sleight of hand. Lory has been inspired to his final exhortation in the courtroom on behalf of personal courage and public resistance to oppression by his accidental witnessing of Professor Sorel's execution. Professor Sorel, it will be remembered, is the publisher of the resistance newspaper. He has been found guilty of sabotage and condemned. As Lory witnesses the preparations of a firing squad from his cell window, his name is called and a close-up registers the shock of recognition. We hear the sound of gunfire offscreen. This execution is so timely—it is the last day of Lory's trial—and the circumstances so improbable as to be a *deus ex machina* to the plot of the film, and it produces an apparent excess in the text of the film.

In consequence, Lory's final speech proffers instant and wholly tendentious moral edification: instant because it is produced *deus ex machina*, tendentious because it does not have value in the *particular* circumstances represented in the film. Renoir may have Lory *argue* the need to act, but he does not embody action in his central character. The particular circumstances in the film that might valorise Lory's advice—and that he himself cites as a model—are the actions of Paul Martin. As the man of action Paul brings about the most spectacular scene of resistance in the film by throwing a bomb in the path of Major von Keller's automobile and assassinating two German soldiers. (Although, since he is photographed from behind during this scene, we are meant to be uncertain of the saboteur's identity.) For his part, Lory remains a passive figure, an outsider who is separated from rather than involved with or acting for society. In the climactic courtroom scenes the very mise-en-scène enforces his estrangement from the townspeople so that he seems to be speaking *to* society rather than *for* society. In this film action and understanding are separated from each other, just as Paul Martin, the man of action, is separated from Albert Lory, the man who achieves understanding. But Martin was never at the narrative centre of the film anyway, and it seems to me that, given the way in which Lory's position as a role model has been achieved *in and by the film*, one has a right to ask whether his assumption of authority has any credibility whatsoever.

The narrative dislocation that necessitates the *deus ex machina* of the resolution indicates a *will* to believe in the possibility of the assumption of authority and influence on the part of an otherwise passive figure. It is what the film wants to assert through the machinery of its plot and through Lory's closing monologue to the court. What is the crisis that lies behind these excesses and dislocations in the film's inscription of meaning? The crisis that sets *This Land Is Mine* in place has been introduced by *La Règle du jeu*, and centres around the characterisation of Octave. Octave is played by Renoir himself.[16] One can note the similarity in physical type between Renoir as Octave at age forty-five and Charles Laughton as Lory at age forty-four—the shambling gait, the overlarge features, a body settling into middle-age corpulence. Accidents of casting, perhaps. Both are inclined to exaggeration: Renoir to wild gestural acting, Laughton to self-indulgent mannerisms. As we have seen, the formal strategies of *La Règle du jeu* permit Octave/Renoir to speak out of character with choric remarks on matters within and without the film. To Lory/Laughton this licence is granted by default of the narrative resolution, so that the address to the court is an address to the audience of the film, enforced by a camera that slavishly concentrates on innumerable frontal medium shots of Lory speaking. Further, if his remarks have not really been justified by the narrative experience of the character, and are not really seen to have value within the quasi-historical experience devised by the film, we are encouraged to see them as a

---

[16] In an interview given in 1939 Renoir admitted the nearly exact resemblance of himself to Octave: "If I wanted to act in it [*La Règle du jeu*], that's because I believe acting constitutes the best school for a director. That's because, after having conceived one of the characters of the film, I recognized that he corresponded to me almost exactly, both physically and morally." See *Image et Son*, no. 282 (March 1974), p. 53.

direct issue from Renoir. This, we conclude, is what *Renoir* wants to say, to us and for himself.

In *La Règle du jeu* Octave is an anxious and insecure figure—a sponger, a failed musician—faced with a morally and politically corrupt society. He knows that society to be corrupt ("We're in a period when everyone tells lies"), knows the hypocrisy and self-interest of its spokesmen ("everyone has their own good reasons"), and knows his helplessness to do anything about it. We can speculate that Octave speaks for Renoir and Renoir's disillusionment at the betrayal of the working-class antifascist causes for which he wrote, argued, and made films from 1935 on. One speculates, too, that through a very self-denigrating character Renoir expresses his own bitterness and despair. We think of the scene with the imaginary orchestra on the steps of the château, of Octave in the moonlight spitting from the little bridge, of the scene with Lisette in the cloakroom in which Octave surveys the implications of his trampled hat. Ironically, it is even he who sacrifices André Jurieu, the one sincere (if clumsy) man who might be the instrument for exposing society's decadence. At the film's end, when Octave accepts his exile from society, he accepts his failure, accepts Renoir's failure to make "contact with the public" through his enormous efforts on behalf of the Popular Front. The very conception of Octave as someone on the margins of society by virtue of his position as an artist-intellectual speaks to the frustrations of the artist become buffoon, the artist as court jester, without a purposeful and instructive function in society.

The socio-political crisis that defines Octave's moral-psychological crisis is also *intended* to define Albert Lory's. The class interests that were served by the internal social corruption examined in *La Règle du jeu* have opened the gates to the political-ideological tyranny from without specified by *This Land Is Mine*. I think this is evident from the conception of Von Keller and his links with La Chesnaye. As for Lory, his cultural privilege, his profession as a schoolteacher, cast him in the mould of Octave's type of bourgeois artist-intellectual. Estranged from society as they are, through situation and character, for both Octave and Lory action is almost impossible. Both men are acted upon. That, I take it, is precisely what depresses Octave about his situation. Unlike Legrand, Toni, Lange, Pepel, even Jacques Lantier, Octave and Lory are the first of Renoir's protagonists incapable of carrying out an action that would define their relationship to society in some positive way. (In the films of the thirties this action is invariably a murder; yet while it is against the law it serves the cause of justice in society by eliminating an influence that threatens either to corrupt or to dissolve community. By comparison, Lory's estrangement is ironically heightened when he is accused of a murder that is in fact a suicide.) Because of the emphasis placed upon his extreme timidity Lory exaggerates Octave's sense of helplessness and self-disgust. One thinks of the scene of his abject confession of fear and ineptitude in Professor Sorel's office following the air raid. Or, more telling as an instance of Lory's paralysis when faced with the need to act is his distinction in the first courtroom scene between the will to courage and his felt cowardice:

> *Lory*: I'm a coward. Everyone knows it, even the prosecutor—that's why he makes fun of me. Oh, I'm not a coward in here. I have brave dreams, I'm not afraid to commit murder *here*—(*Touching his head*)—but when I face reality outside I'm lost, I'm a coward. It's so strange. We're two people, all of us. One inside and one outside.[17]

That there is some (perhaps unwitting) intention on Renoir's part to grant both Octave and Lory a similar awareness of their common situations is indicated by nearly identical lines of dialogue applied to each of them:

[17] *This Land Is Mine*, p. 867.

Robert: You know, you're not an idiot, you're a poet, a dangerous poet![18]

Von Keller: You're a poet, Lory. A poet![19]

But the fact remains that while it is given to Octave and eventually to Lory to perceive the situations with which they are confronted, neither is capable of acting in political and social arenas. And while Octave is honestly shown not to have any influence whatsoever, the influence that is thrust upon Albert Lory has not been earned and cannot be taken seriously.

Faced with social corruption and political oppression, what is the bourgeois artist-intellectual to do? When Lory echoes Octave's anxiety at discriminating "what's good, and what's bad," it seems to me that he restates Renoir's frustration in *La Règle du jeu* at reaching out to his social class and cultural peers:

> *Lory*: It's very hard for people like you and me to understand what is evil and what is good. It's easy for working people to know who the enemy is because the aim of this War and this Occupation is to make them slaves. But middle class people like us can easily believe as George Lambert did—that a German victory isn't such a bad thing.[20]

As a committed film maker during the thirties, Renoir devoted his best efforts to the transformation of society through an alliance of the middle and working classes. By the end of the decade he despaired of change and expressed his disillusionment with the presumption of influence and authority on the part of the bourgeois artist-intellectual. By 1943, at the time of the making of *This Land Is Mine*, perhaps Renoir is no more confident of what the role of the artist-intellectual should be, since

[18] Jean Renoir, *Rules of the Game*, trans. John McGrath and Maureen Teitelbaum (New York: Simon and Schuster, 1970), p. 55.

[19] *This Land Is Mine*, p. 869.

[20] Ibid., p. 871.

he must force the resolution of his film in order that he may *will* Lory's assumption of authority. Divorced as they are from any meaningful context within the film, Lory's remarks to the court—such as those quoted immediately above—constitute the film as a moralising discourse. On the evidence of the films behind him, or of the films to come, that is not a practice with which Renoir has ever been very satisfied. For the moment, however, and for the next few years, he cannot see his way clear to changing his practice. The artistic crisis articulated by *La Règle du jeu* and rephrased by *This Land Is Mine* will not be resolved until Renoir's trip to India to make *The River*. Then, in the great colour films of the fifties, in *The Golden Coach* and *French Cancan* particularly, and in his biography of his father, Renoir will have realised a new role for the artist and a new function for art to carry him through his second maturity.

Before we get to Renoir's work of the fifties there is one more film to be examined in some detail, a film that represents a necessary intermediate stage out of his first maturity and into his second. *The Southerner* anticipates a major ideological and epistemological shift in Renoir's career, a shift that is obscured if one seeks to understand the film by grasping at what it may have in common with earlier films. In a very important sense Renoir is starting again from zero in the United States. The films of his American period are films of transition for Renoir. With *This Land Is Mine* he has one foot in the thirties; with *The Southerner* he has his other foot in the fifties. I want to discuss *The Southerner* because I want to make a sharp distinction between its qualities and those of the prewar films—a distinction worth making sharply because it is a film frequently confused with those earlier works, when it actually looks forward to *The River*.

If criticism usually considers *The Southerner* Renoir's best American film, that is surely because it is his most American film, fitting neatly into determinedly (and determined) American ideological-generic structures. *The Southerner* is first of all fed

by the great generic river that is the American cinema—not by
the Renoir films heretofore—and the generic code is value-laden
a priori. As a version of the American pastoral one can begin
to understand *The Southerner* by looking at the structural com-
monplaces it shares with other films of the New Deal, sharecropper type, from *Our Daily Bread* (1934) to *The Grapes of Wrath*
(1940).[21] *The Southerner* is first of all a film in this genre, then
it is a film directed by Renoir. What is fascinating for criticism
is how Renoir conducts his own naturalization of the ideological
imperatives of the genre. For the moment, I think it is important
to insist that the generic code was there for Renoir to inherit
the instant he embarked on his adaptation for the cinema of
George Sessions Perry's novel *Hold Autumn in Your Hand*: the
socially constructed thematics of the code preexist their particular
use in *The Southerner*. Looked at synchronically, *The Southerner*
shares with other films of its type a binary system of oppositional
sets that codifies the narrative. The country/town opposition is
primary; all other sets follow from this in an associative series.
These can be listed in descending order to some particularities
of *The Southerner*; the terms in each set are opposed to one
another along the thematic axis of the text. In practice, many

---

[21] Historically, of course, *The Southerner* is not a film of the New Deal, but post facto
it cannot escape generic influences from the thirties. I confess to being uncertain as to
whether the historical setting of *The Southerner* is intended to be 1944-1945, the time
at which it was made, or the end of the thirties. At one point in the film Sam and Tim
walk past a cinema where *Vogues of 1938* (1937), *One Rainy Afternoon* (1936), and
Intermezzo (American version, 1939) are all advertised. Perhaps the titles merely verify
the delinquency of distributors in getting films to backwoods cinemas. On the other
hand, if *The Southerner* were clearly to announce the period of its setting, that would
give it an historical specificity it probably does not want. The novel from which it was
adapted, *Hold Autumn in Your Hand* by George Sessions Perry, was published in January
1941 by Viking Press, but the text does not specify the historical time frame, either. In
any case, *The Southerner* belongs to a genre of the American pastoral whose New Deal
representatives include *Our Daily Bread* and *The Grapes of Wrath*. The pastoral has a
long tradition in American cinema and a catalogue would have to include, among others,
Tol'able David (King, 1921), *The Wind* (Seastrom, 1927), *Sunrise* (Murnau, 1927), *City
Girl* (Murnau, 1928), *Of Mice and Men* (Milestone, 1939), *Tobacco Road* (Ford, 1941),
and *The Yearling* (Brown, 1946).

of the terms are read iconographically, inasmuch as they have
to do with place, dress, food, and signify moral attitude, social
condition, and so on:

country	town
family	individual
settlement	rootlessness
wife	whore
love	sex
spirituality	materiality
self-sufficiency	dependency
poverty	wealth
barter	consumerism
farm	factory
work	talk
hands	machines
earth	metal
open-neck shirt	tie and jacket
water, milk	beer, liquor

Clearly, the sets in the above code—and they can be extended
ad infinitum—are transferable to any film within which this
system of relations can be discovered.[22]

[22] The idea for laying out the code in this way and with some of these structural
oppositions comes from Sam Rohdie's analysis of *Mr. Deeds Goes to Town* in his "Totems
and Movies," in *Movies and Methods*, ed. Bill Nichols (Berkeley and Los Angeles:
University of California Press, 1976), pp. 469-480. If there is something distressingly
facile about such naked structuralism, as Rohdie points out, I suspect that is because
these sets *are* transferable to a great many films in classical American cinema. In fact,
this binary system may constitute a basic code—the deep structure, as it were—for much
of that cinema. The associations in the series may be extended, or modified, or split off
into new compound variants to accommodate many Westerns, *film noir*, horror films,
melodramas, and so on. Robin Wood, for example, has done his own structural analysis
of the common ideological tensions at work in *It's a Wonderful Life* and *Shadow of a
Doubt* in his "Ideology, Genre, Auteur," *Film Comment* 13, no. 1 (1977), pp. 46-51.

Now, if we are to escape the banality of otherwise inert classification, it seems very
much to the point that we should remember that we are talking about a generic code
that is value-laden. So far as American cinema is concerned, this code—much refined

The dynamism for the oppositional sets or thematic elements that constitute the generic code is initially provided by plot, which from film to film in any generic series will play with the same structural oppositions but with differing narrative articulations. To be precise about reading the operation of the generic code, other, specifically cinematic codes would also have to be invoked: lighting, editing, composition and framing, camera. Finally, then, how the terms that constitute the sets operate in tension or conflict will vary from film to film. The point is that the meaning or value of the code is as much a matter of form as it is of content: it is determined by a total system of signification.[23] Use of the code in classical American cinema is not in itself a matter of choice for the film maker, only the formal inflection he will give it (although that, too, has its highly conventionalized practices, and is not, therefore, divorced from an historical conjuncture). Above all, that means that Jean Renoir in 1946 is not going to produce the same text as King Vidor in 1934 or John Ford in 1940. Precisely because the formal inflection

to accept further differences and resemblances—may represent a significant aspect of its ideological representation of social reality. This is how Americans have represented to themselves who and what they are through their cinema. Once American social reality has been codified in this way, what is expressed by drawing on this system ensures the preservation of that reality. And in so far as contradiction is limited by the familiar signifying practices of classical, illusionist narrative, that reality will become the "truth" in support of the existing social formation. The sheer repetition of this code through various cinematic genres is crucial to the successful naturalization of an ideologically determined social reality.

Not that such a general observation says a great deal in itself. It says that such a code is at work and that it has an important ideological determination, but it does not say anything useful about how it works diachronically through a series of texts or about how it works in a particular text. There is always the danger of placing too much speculative weight on a series of abstract relations at the expense of *particular* analysis. The table of thematic elements in the generic code cannot honestly be said to be the meaning of *The Southerner*, or of any other film, since it stands quite apart from any particular narrative operation or influential historical conditions. But I am not about to attempt a full-scale theoretical discussion of the conjunction history/ideology/genre. I am interested in establishing Renoir's dependence upon a generic code and the ideological determinations that support it.

[23] This is Rohdie's insistence too: "Totems and Movies," especially pp. 473-474.

is primarily his responsibility, the film maker will dynamise the code out of its inertness and abstraction into the aesthetic performance of a particular film.

To address the film itself let me begin with a difference (from Renoir's films of the thirties) and a resemblance (to other films of its type). Although it has been observed (by Raymond Durgnat, I believe) that *The Southerner* is the first film directed by Renoir to deal with a family, that is not because Renoir has taken a sudden personal interest in family life, but because the family is ideologically the most important social unit in American cinema. That the family does not figure in Renoir's films of the thirties verifies the principal ideological engagement of the French films as class-directed. Ideologically, the presence and meaning of the family in *The Southerner* is inexorably determined by those same ideological-generic structures to which other film makers in America are subject.

It is a truism to say that classical American cinema celebrates the family. Consanguinity is stronger than any other bond—stronger than class, race, or religion. When Tom Joad must leave the government camp in *The Grapes of Wrath*, Ma's lament is that the family is "crackin' up," even though Tom himself may be moved by a vague social activism. The solidarity of any collective enterprise (as in *Our Daily Bread*) is only as secure as its elemental units: the individual families. Work may (sometimes) be done cooperatively, but social existence is defined familially, not communally. Always in American cinema it is the family that valorizes man as a social creature and a complete human being, not class. If the films in the New Deal sharecropper genre ultimately fail to subvert established political and economic interests, that is in part because they are consistently sentimental (family) rather than materialist (class). To be able or willing to talk about social relations in terms of class might be to expose some of the contradictions of capitalism by perceiving the social formation in a way that could contest its institutions and ideology. Inasmuch as the intimate portrayal of the family in *The*

Grapes of Wrath arouses sentimental feelings in the spectator at the expense of social analysis, we are rendered passive and impotent, and any correction of a general situation of class exploitation is impossible. In this way films defeat the prospect of change, and in consequence (if not in intention) preserve the dominant ideology.

The importance of the family to films of this type is supported by the example of Devers (J. Carroll Naish) in *The Southerner*, who is a rigorous instance of self-help so far as work is concerned, but otherwise socially and morally pitiable (but not condemnable). More than the traditional ideal of good-neighbourliness is at issue in Devers's clash with Sam (Zachary Scott). His refusal of milk for the ailing Jotty or his destruction of the vegetable patch seem to me to aim at no less than the breakup of the Tucker family. Devers's farm may be rich and flourishing, but he is personally bitter and morally stunted, apparently because the hardships of sharecropping have cost him the lives of his wife and son. However, he directs his anger towards Sam out of envy rather than towards "the system" out of any critical awareness of the historical reasons for his loss. In fact Devers's loss (and Sam's hardship) is due to the social exploitation of landholders like Ruston. But directing Devers's anger and frustration towards Sam enables the film to mystify the extent of Ruston's responsibility in favour of our moral judgement of Devers as having failed the ideal of good-neighbourliness. Ruston remains an intangible presence, and "hard luck" becomes the cause of Devers's reprehensible behaviour. That Devers is placated in the course of the film—as just another natural hardship for Sam to overcome—is one way in which *The Southerner* closes contradiction and fully secures the personalisation of a wide-scale social situation of class dimensions. The ideological work of *The Southerner* is as subtle as that of *The Grapes of Wrath*.

In the family structure it is the wife who anchors the home as a site of value and as a system of social relations. (Is not one of the most moving scenes in *The Grapes of Wrath* that in which Ma Joad sits by the small fire in her empty house destroying mementoes of the sentimental history of her family—and its material history, as well, if she only knew it?) As we see from the example of Devers, when the wife is absent that system breaks down and man becomes an antisocial and incomplete human being. The function of the wife (or mother) is nearly identical in the trio of *Our Daily Bread, The Grapes of Wrath*, and *The Southerner*: an endlessly suffering, always dependable helpmate; the embodiment of domesticity; a loving companion in a relationship denied any eroticism or evidence of sexual activity beyond procreation of the family. The wife's virtues, like her role, are decidedly Christian and conservative. And if she is sometimes nearly invisible in this intensely patriarchal cinema, that is because she is an adjunct to the male protagonist, a steady beacon in the storm he must weather, there to remind him by word or example of his one true goal.

The protagonist must constantly suppress the temptation to surrender the struggle for a better, more equitable life on his terms. Although there may be any number of obstacles to self-fulfilment in classical American cinema, the most frequent temptation to waywardness appears in the guise of wanton sexuality, inasmuch as any sexual activity is seen to be incompatible with home, family, work, dignity, authority (see just about everything from *The Birth of a Nation* to *Citizen Kane*). Wanton sexuality is embodied by the whore, sometimes thrown in the way of the protagonist at the lowest point in his fortunes when he is most vulnerable (*Our Daily Bread*). Her iconography is familiar, from the factitious luxury of makeup and fashion to the unrefined vocal accents of city streets. But unlike the wives in *Our Daily Bread* and *The Southerner*, the women identified as whores function quite differently, or at least they function towards a somewhat different end in the case of each film, a difference that helps to distinguish and thereby particularize the two works.

In *Our Daily Bread* the success of the cooperative depends

upon the moral integrity of the protagonist, John. In him are
vested the responsibilities of leadership, so that through speech,
but above all through action, he is a model to the other members
of the group. For the cooperative to succeed his authority must
remain inviolable. Since internal strife among the group is min-
imal and quickly eradicated, neither the erosion of John's authority nor social disintegration begin until the arrival of Sally,
the sexual temptress. And although she is warned away from
John, he gradually becomes more and more distracted, by her
and by the lure of money and excitement and travel that she
promises. The low point of fortune for the co-op is the drought,
a disaster that is natural but that in some sense has a moral cause
since it is coincident with Sally's increasing sway over John.
Only when he rejects the temptation of Sally can he muster the
community to divert water to the parched cornfield, thereby
restoring his authority and re-uniting the collective. It is worth
remarking that the solution to the drought is revealed to John
even while he is on the road away from the farm with Sally.
She drives on; he returns to save himself, his family, and the
cooperative. The issue here is that the presence and the importance of Sally as a highly codified type of the female who appears
throughout American cinema indicates that John's trial—and
through him the security of his family and the ordeal of the
cooperative—is entirely moral rather than vaguely social (*The
Grapes of Wrath*) or spiritual (*The Southerner*). (Unlike Sam
Tucker or Tom Joad, John's origins are in the city, so that in
a way this moral trial is undergone to prove his country-wor-
thiness and purify him of city attachments.) The cooperative as
a putative social formation can only be validated by John's moral
victory. And not only Sally, but Louie, the wanted criminal,
must also leave the community if it is to succeed. All will be
right with the world socially if we are all of us true morally.
Moral truth in this case means the values of a thoroughgoing
Christian humanism. This means, finally, that in the interests
of promoting collective enterprise *Our Daily Bread* masks any

potential contradiction with the historical reality of 1934. Focusing on the John–Sally conflict as the principal obstacle to narrative closure has obviated the necessity for the film to confront those historical conditions that might challenge its utopian social formation and its Edenic view of the land (i.e., America).

An equivalent figure of the whore also appears in *The Southerner*. Unlike Sally's relationship to John in *Our Daily Bread*, however, the type of the whore in *The Southerner* whom Sam meets in the town saloon does not figure in a moral trial for him. She is there to centre his values more squarely in our minds over against those of Tim (played by Charles Kemper), town and factory. Tim, who is Sam's distant cousin, works in the city and continually argues the advantage of a guaranteed daily wage as the solution to Sam's frustrated efforts to wrench a living from the earth to support his family. The town whore belongs to Tim's world, not Sam's, and her temptation of Sam is a failure from the start. To Tim, on the other hand, she is property to be bought and used. The opposition of the country and the town in *The Southerner* is a polarity without tension, so that the signification "town" and its associations can point up by comparison the positive value of the signification "country" and its associations. After all, Sam maintains his friendship with Tim— dressed in suit and tie, flashing money and liquor like any "success story"—throughout the film.

In town one is assured a guaranteed wage and consumer power, but one must serve as "somebody else's man," to use Sam's words. That we never see Tim at work—he talks mostly and seems basically sedentary, rather heavy and slow—suggests that his work is somehow unfulfilling. What this means by implicit comparison with the country is that work in a factory is not assumed to be a good in itself: (a) because the relations of production involve the division of labour; and (b) because the worker is deprived of owning the means of production; consequently (c) he never realises the product of his labour except as wages (even as surplus wages); so that (d) money alone can

153

be shown to be an insufficient reward for work done (i.e., Tim does not have a family or a wife, a home or roots). Of course, for ideological purposes the film represents Tim's situation less analytically by refusing any examination of (a), (b), or (c) in order to emphasise (d) to the sentimental advantage of Sam. Its declared judgement, however, is that the cash gained as the price of wage labour has a generally deleterious effect: *because* Tim earns seven dollars a day in a factory he is swindled by the bartender and a woman of questionable virtue, which initiates the most violent scene in the film, a scene that takes care to show us the large-scale destruction of property. While Tim protests that with money in his pocket he is free, he (and his world) measure all things and all people by what they cost: "What the heck you got that I can't buy with my dough?"

Sam, whose freedom is in working on the land, does not think of property in terms like Tim's, he thinks in terms of self-sufficiency for himself and his family. Rather conveniently, however, the film allows us to forget that title to Sam's farm belongs to Ruston. His freedom and self-sufficiency are something of an illusion since he does not own his means of production. But the film is not weighted so as to question the interests of capital; it is content to celebrate a personal idealism. In the American cinema the celebration of personal idealism is the commonest ideological tactic for mystifying the operations of corporate capitalism, even though as here, despite the *real* social positions of Sam and Tim, it may be necessary to mask the most obvious contradictions. Neither Tim nor Sam is actually free, then, for both have sold their labour power to capital interests. What the film does is obscure the real production relations in Sam's case so that his will may *seem* to be free, and expose them in Tim's case so that his existence can be seen to depend upon commodity relations. It is essential to what I take to be the spiritual idealism of the film that we continue to believe Sam free, that what is in fact an ideological practice be read as natural.

Again, the opposition between commodity relations and human relations emerges as a commonplace (and contradictory) thematic of American cinema, and in *Our Daily Bread, The Grapes of Wrath*, and *The Southerner* it is just as much associated with two kinds of place as it is with two kinds of women, or two kinds of labour, or two kinds of social existence. That wage labour has the power to destroy home, family, and personal relations is superbly illustrated by Muley's flashback in *The Grapes of Wrath*. The tractor that arrives to level his house, break up the family unit, and push Muley off his land is driven by a neighbour who pleads the necessity of three dollars a day. Suited and goggled, the neighbour is the dehumanized extension of his machine. An awesome thing, it is shown in close, low-angled shots moving across the landscape like an insensate monster. Here, and to a lesser extent in *The Southerner*, the wages of corporate capitalism (banks, cattle companies, cotton monopolies, factories) are linked to industrial technology, over against the values of a virtual preindustrial relationship to the land in which man labours in direct physical contact with the nourishing soil. "My dirt," says Grandpa Joad, running it through his fingers. But, as I have already suggested, for ideological reasons the opposition is almost entirely sentimental since the operations of corporate capitalism are never analyzed while downtrodden man is idealised. The emotional commitment to an idealist view of human existence is so powerful in these films ("We're the people") that it not only prevents opposition to the interests of capital from becoming politically articulate, it renders opposition impotent, thereby further securing the dominance and perpetuation of those interests. The myth is that in the country, on the land, the penniless, who "don't answer to nobody" (*The Southerner*), in the dignity of their self-sufficient labour are the pure in heart. This ideological masquerade is designed to obviate the possibility of any transformation of society. In *The Southerner* the independent initiative of the Tucker family is rewarded with a good cotton crop whose value is not to be measured by money alone, for their shared toil has a qualitative human worth.

The Southerner deals with the hardships of the labouring man, but not in social terms, rather, as I have suggested, in "human" terms. Perhaps, then, it would be more accurate to say that *The Southerner* deals with the "human" problems of a man and his family who happen to be of the rural working class. I suspect that is what critics mean when they describe the film as "lyrical" Renoir. *The Southerner* is not much interested in social reality, but in an essentialist, "inner" reality that transcends historical conditions of time and place. I suspect that the film's *vraisemblable*, earned partly by virtue of its location shooting, is merely a generic factor, unrecognized by those otherwise attentive to its idealism. (Eric Rohmer: "There is no trace in this quasi-documentary of the customary Hollywood production.")[24] This quasi-documentary practice *is* consistent with Hollywood's illusionist standards for a film in this genre. Certainly there is not the dialectical play here between realism and truth, between the camera and the environment, such as effects the socialization of space in *Toni* or in the opening sequence of *Boudu sauvé des eaux*. *The Southerner* does not purport to have a social conscience. It is not a populist work in any sense—politically or journalistically—that is at all concerned with seeking economic justice for the sharecroppers of the southern United States. Sam *is* an exploited figure—his freedom is as illusory as Tim's—but that exploitation is not absolutely denied by the film anymore than it is attacked. Let us say that it is *noticed*, in the presence of Ruston, then ignored, to the disadvantage of the film's historical reality but to the advantage of what it values. Despite the fact that we know Sam and his labour to be exploited, the images of the film show him labouring with conventional dignity, doubtless to the profit of a society that we are supposed to accept as it is.

Although exposing Sam's exploitation is not the purpose of the film, perhaps *The Southerner* is more honest than *Our Daily*

---

[24] See André Bazin, *Jean Renoir* (New York: Simon and Schuster, 1973), p. 269.

Bread, say, in noticing it and not denying it, or, worse, euphe-
mizing it by supposing it can somehow be made to disappear—
out of sight out of mind—by socialistic production relations
within a capitalist state. In this the naiveté of *Our Daily Bread*
is more patent than that of *The Southerner*. I believe Vidor's
recourse to euphemism is apparent from the images of work in
his film. I am thinking of that final sequence of the digging of
the irrigation ditch, in which the shots of the files of men wield-
ing shovel or pick are artfully choreographed and composed to
produce the monumentalism of friezes. In the longer shots, with
their consistently low angles, the composition balances the men
in the frame, frequently posing them between earth and sky.
Eisenstein is usually invoked when this sequence is mentioned,
but Dovzhenko seems to me its true precursor both in style and
idea, since its force does not lie in montage. These images aestheticize work, and aestheticize man's triumph over Nature, so
that what we regard is not the work itself but a paean to the
ethic of work and the taming of the land. That is what *Our
Daily Bread* would promote. This cannot be said of *The Southerner*, even though the images of Sam at work in the fields are
as much a part of this film's centre of value as Vidor's images
are of his.

What is it that *The Southerner* appears to value? The country
is represented as redemptive, and not especially in terms of the
ethics of work—for that is finally an ancillary theme—but in
terms of being in touch with the rhythms of Nature: "the factory
hides your [God's] sky and puts out your light," says Sam. To
emphasize this theme of man's relationship to the ever-renewing
cycle of Nature, Renoir has built his narrative on the passing of
the seasons. A calendar motif is even used to introduce each
season in turn: Autumn–Winter–Spring–Autumn. Stylistically,
too, each season is distinctive. The exterior shots of early autumn
and spring tend to be longer and more open, showing considerable depth, and frequently marked by a strong horizon line,
like the right-to-left camera movements across the cotton rows

in the opening scene, or the shots from the porch of the house with Sam plowing far down in the field. As the year moves into late autumn, shots are less open, compositions more closed, with the characters often framed by other objects in the image—a tree or the house—and placed against a near and recognizable background, unlike the wide spaces of springtime. The few winter scenes are claustrophobic since both interiors and exteriors are relatively dark, the exteriors almost flat and two-dimensional as Sam hunts the possum through the swirling mist. The interiors feel close since the camera cannot move or show much depth in the dim space of the Tuckers' shack. I think these stylistic differences in the treatment of the changing year are an important aspect of our *felt* experience of the family's situation. One must sense the immensity of a superior force, on whose rhythms man depends, even while he is at their mercy. This desperate tension is marvellously caught by two successive shots in the film, shots that are both contrasting and complementary. In her despair at Jotty's spring-sickness Nona (Betty Field) throws herself face-down upon the reluctant earth, the camera tilted down at her full length exposed in the open field. Following a quick linking shot, the next shot is a slight upward angle of Sam's head and shoulders against an empty sky as he prays to God for support. It is just this emphasis on the relationship of man to earth and sky, of man to the natural cycle, that confirms the film's commitment to a nonsocial "inner" reality beyond particular circumstances of time and place.

When we are introduced to the Tucker family at the start of the film there is no historical account of the reasons for their poverty. Similarly, in the course of the film, as they suffer one adversity after another—hunger, sickness, the personal enmity of Devers, natural disaster—these hardships seem a matter of bad luck rather than the consequences of a definable social structure. Sam's misfortunes are those of Job rather than of history—a test of his faith—unsolicited, and relieved by no intervention of his own. The family needs milk to ward off the dreaded pellagra. Sam stands in the field and prays for a sign. In the next scene Tim arrives with a cow. It might be argued as a weakness of the film that we are asked to accept the family's blessings as given, or else produced by the unaccountable intercession of some *deus ex machina*. But I do not think this is so. I think they are earned *on the terms set by the film*, earned by the images of perseverance through work, of endurance through suffering, and of conviction through faith, however mystifying historically we may take these images to be. They are earned by what I can only call the spiritual trial of the Tucker family. The film wants to affirm certain values—the strength that comes from endurance, the necessity of faith—and what serves to call them into question is not some moral frailty of the protagonist (as in *Our Daily Bread*), or historically defined social circumstances (as in *The Grapes of Wrath*), but what we are persuaded to believe is the universal condition of man.

If we are to accept that the film affirms these values successfully, we must respond positively to the formal authority of its images and to the emotional directness of the characters and character relationships. In none of the characters or their relationships with one another is there anything like the emotional complexity of Renoir's films of the thirties, with their personal and class conflicts leading to murder and social disturbance (the tormented Michel Legrand of *La Chienne*, lovesick Toni, the fantastic M. Lange, the adolescent confusions of *Partie de campagne*, the enigmatic Baron and smouldering Pepel of *Les Bas-Fonds*, ill-fated Jacques Lantier, troubled Octave). Against the emotional turmoil we recall from the earlier films we would have to place the understated scene of straightforward affection between Sam and Nona when he sits on the edge of their makeshift bed and rolls her a cigarette at the end of their first evening in their new home. Throughout the film the quiet credibility of Zachary Scott's performance as Sam deserves to be singled out.[25] Sam is shown to have the same ingenuous belief

[25] James Agee, whom one might expect to be a helpful judge, found that Scott's

in the superstition that vegetables cause pellagra as he does in the natural "signs," or in God. When he offers God thanks for a meal, it is a simple "Much obliged, Lord." When he stands in the field and appeals to God for support, the appeal is not for—and makes no contract for—redemption out of time. It is still the turning of the year to which Sam is bound; the existence of God is not a function of Renoir's metaphysic but of Sam's character. While Sam's appeal to God might seem to be the climax of the film since it is followed by the arrival of the cow, reconciliation with Devers, a good cotton crop, and the marriage of Harmie and Ma, the real climax is the flood that wastes all Sam's effort in one night of rain. This is Sam's final test, for there is to be no compensatory happy ending. The marriage festival of Harmie and Ma suggests the resolution of the mythos of comedy (Northrop Frye), but with the unexpected flood the film goes on to take another shape, a shape we might reservedly call divine comedy. This represents an important narrative strategy on Renoir's part, for without this development we would be manipulated into favouring the shallowest kind of idealism. Instead, the film asks us to value humility more than arrogance and to recognize that what is humanly desired is not necessarily true. *The Southerner* is a great deal less utopian in its view of community and much more guarded in its idealism than *Our Daily Bread* or some other films in the genre. This caution is expressed visually as well by the last few images of the film, as the family surveys the damage to home and crops caused by the flood. Shot after static shot is tightly framed with dark borders and a clutter of objects in the space surrounding the characters to convey the constraint upon the spirit produced by this devastation. If the family does endure through all adversity, they do so finally because of an inner strength born of their acqui-

---

performance alone conveyed an exemplary naturalism: "The one person in the film who for all his minor mistakes is basically right, in everything from cheekbones and eyes to posture to spiritual attitude, is Zachary Scott; he was born in Texas." Agee's review is reprinted in *Agee on Film* (New York: McDowell, Obolensky, 1958), pp. 166-168.

escence in a cycle of creation and destruction that is superior to the will of man. "I'm beginning to believe again," says Sam at the film's conclusion, when he sees his family rebuilding after the flood. The cycle is completed in the actions of the characters as Sam props up the porch and the stove is lit once again, repeating the first scene of the family's arrival at the farm. The final two-shot of Sam and Nona, the tight-framing having been relaxed, does suggest that stability and faith have been restored with modesty. This shot is quite unlike the celebratory group shots that conclude *Our Daily Bread*. It is closer to the last, tight shots of Ma and Pa Joad in the truck at the end of *The Grapes of Wrath*, but without the resolve carried by the fact that the truck is moving or by Ma's words ("We're the people!"). Sam and Nona stand together on the earth before the newly plowed field. This shot of them signifies nothing more nor less than their inner certitude. To accept the congruity of human life with Nature's rhythms—what Sam does at the end—is to be at one with an essential mystery at the heart of all living things.

For the first time in Renoir's work natural processes are emphasised at the expense of historical processes, and that indicates a major ideological shift, which will be verified with *The River*. The sentimental humanism of *The Southerner* has nothing to do with the social consciousness of Renoir's prewar films. If *The Southerner* remains a capable film but not an astonishing film, that is because Renoir does not explore, or does not recognize, the contradictions and tensions inherent in his codified debts to genre and ideology. At the same time, I have shown something of the extent to which Renoir has brought a stylistic authority to his particular naturalization of the ideological imperatives of the genre. On into the maturity of his second career in the fifties Renoir will re-form the limits of genre to direct two great works with *The Golden Coach* and *French Cancan*.

FOUR

AN IDEOLOGY OF AESTHETICS:
THE RIVER, THE GOLDEN COACH,
FRENCH CANCAN

HARRIET: *We go on as if nothing had happened!*
MOTHER: *No, we don't. We just go on.*

THE RIVER

Against the claim that "Renoir's films add up to one immensely rich and varied single work,"[1] I have argued that Jean Renoir has had two distinct careers. These two careers are distinguished by different functions for art and different roles for the artist. It is that second career, that second maturity as a film maker, to which I now want to address myself. The films of this second maturity, eight features over eighteen years, from *The River* (1951) to *Le Petit théâtre de Jean Renoir* (1969), demonstrate new thematic concerns and new stylistic preoccupations consistent with Renoir's self-confessed change in attitude towards art and life.

However, I do not think that the epistemological and ideological shift, as I have called it, that produced this functional difference in Renoir's two careers came about abruptly. *La Règle du jeu,* made on the eve of the Second World War, clearly indicates Renoir's frustration at his inability to act in the interests of social change through its portrait of Octave the failed artist. Tensions in the film's processes of signification produce excesses in the text, which create its disparaging interpretation of contemporary society. And what I have called the artistic crisis of

[1] Peter Harcourt, *Six European Directors* (Harmondsworth: Penguin Books, 1974), p. 68.

This Land Is Mine is a (more or less unconscious) crisis in ideological perspective, which I have posed as a question concerning the responsibilities of the bourgeois artist-intellectual in the face of Renoir's flight from defeated France. I have argued that this crisis is symptomatically present in the text of the film through the forced narrative closure brought about by the *deus ex machina* of Professor Sorel's timely execution, an unexpected structuration of the text that has the troubling effect of insecurely willing Lory's ability to act productively with his assumption of influence and authority in the final courtroom scene. With *The Southerner*, however, made at the end of the Second World War and after Renoir had spent five years in the United States, we have a new ideological perspective in evidence. The tenacious survival of the Tucker family urges that we recognize certain essential human values in bowing to the necessary congruity of human life with Nature's rhythms. This is a philosophy at once more idealist and less historically informed than anything Renoir's films have proposed before.[2]

The River, too, ignores historical processes to celebrate a timeless cycle of creation and destruction. That *The Southerner* anticipates the ideological and philosophical shift which is finally complete with *The River* may also be supported by the fact that Renoir's interest in Rumer Godden's novel goes back to 1946, although *The River* was not released until 1951. It was little better than a year after the release of *The Southerner*, in other

---

[2] While it may be objected that there are earlier films directed by Renoir which give precedence to Nature, I do not think this is so. Certainly there are films in which the environment represented is a vital element, as with the sequence in the park at the opening of *Boudu sauvé des eaux*, the mountainscapes in *La Grande Illusion*, or the countryside in *Toni* and *La Règle du jeu*. But the natural settings in these examples are at the service of character definition in films whose primary concern is social conflict. This seems to me no less true of *Partie de campagne*, although we have the film only in an abbreviated version, and even of *La Bête humaine*, despite the fact that its essentialist psychology makes it an activist film *manqué*. In none of these films does the whole natural cycle represent the well-defined, philosophical idealism that it does in *The Southerner* or *The River*.

words, that his interest in the book was stirred by a review in *The New Yorker*. Since *The River* has its genesis in the middle of Renoir's American period, one should not be surprised to find some continuity between his new ideological perspective in the United States and the full reconstitution of consciousness in evidence from this film. By refusing to engage at all with the social, political, or economic implications of the post-Independence Western presence in India, *The River* completes a gradual shift away from subject matter that deals with specific historical realities. With the films of Renoir's second maturity, it is the world of art that offers us the individual and collective dream of social harmony fulfilled.

In view of the informing role of art in human experience that is granted by the films of the fifties, it is worth pointing to the recognition that Renoir takes of his father, for the first time in his career, just months after the completion of shooting on *This Land Is Mine*. In 1943 Renoir wrote an introduction to an exhibition of his father's paintings at a Los Angeles gallery.[3] Since that time Renoir has mentioned his father lovingly and often,

---

[3] Jean Renoir, [Introduction], *Renoir (1841-1919)* (Los Angeles: Dalzell Hatfield Galleries, 1943). During the late twenties and throughout the thirties Renoir seems deliberately to have suppressed his paternity, since I have not found the slightest reference to Pierre-Auguste Renoir in any of Renoir's writings, interviews, or films for those years. Support for this view may be found in *My Life and My Films* (New York: Atheneum, 1974), p. 100, "I have spent my life trying to determine the extent of the influence of my father upon me, passing over the periods when I did my utmost to escape from it to dwell upon those when my mind was filled with the precepts I thought I had gleaned from him." Incidentally, the introduction to this gallery exhibition of 1943 may not be quite the first recognition Renoir accords his father. One or two shots in *Swamp Water* (1941) of the character Jesse Wick (played by John Carradine) in his bunk clearly show an illustration of a Renoir painting tacked to the wall!

Criticism took no special notice of Renoir's paternity during the thirties either, not until Roger Leenhardt's 1946 essay, "Jean Renoir et la tradition française," in *Intermède*, no. 1 (Spring 1946), pp. 102-110. Since 1950, however, critics have talked of the influence of Pierre-Auguste or of Impressionism upon Renoir, often reading backwards from *Renoir, My Father* for an interpretation of Renoir's career up to 1939 or drawing upon images in the films (although *La Balançoire*, for example, has no genuine resemblance to any shot in *Partie de campagne*).

for this first piece was followed by a number of others through the ensuing years, to be crowned by the appearance of the biography *Renoir, My Father* in 1962.[4] These writings are a valuable adjunct to the work in film and an important complementary source of ideas concerning art and the artist. I do not mean that the stated precepts on aesthetic matters in the biography are necessarily to be historically attributed to Pierre-Auguste Renoir, or that the position of the films of the fifties is a direct consequence of paternal influence. After all, Pierre-Auguste's "cork theory," offered by Renoir in the biography as an explanation of his father's attitude towards life, is simply another metaphor for Renoir's own so-called philosophy of acceptance. Perhaps in this, as in other matters, Renoir has actually influenced his father rather more than he thought. Renoir has warned us of the likelihood, in the headnote to the biography:

> *The Reader*: It is not Renoir you are presenting to us, but your own conception of him.
>
> *The Author*: Of course, History is a subjective genre, after all.[5]

What *Renoir, My Father* offers us, on his own implicit acknowledgement, is Renoir's conception of himself. Quite transparently, *Renoir, My Father* is actually two interwoven chronicles, biography and autobiography, about two lives, father and son. The first is a marvellous, vital evocation of French domestic and social life through the latter half of the nineteenth century. At the same time, the achronological and anecdotal structure of the book, apparently out of respect for the disorder of Pierre-Au-

[4] Prior to the publication of the biography Renoir wrote "My Memories of Renoir," for *Life* (19 May 1952), pp. 90-99, and "My Father's Sunset Years,"*Art News* 57, no. 2 (April 1958), pp. 38-40, both of which appeared in a slightly different form in *Renoir, My Father*. He also wrote the introduction for an exhibition of his father's work in Paris in 1954, and again for a Paris exhibition of 1955. After 1962, he did similar honours in 1964, 1969, and 1973.

[5] *Renoir, My Father* (Boston: Little, Brown, 1962), p. v.

guste's reminiscences as first jotted down by Renoir in 1915, encourages the author to single out from a myriad of incidents and maxims those that emphasise continuity with his own life. It would appear that Renoir began his biography of his father about 1952, shortly after he completed *The River*; consequently the philosophy it espouses (moral, aesthetic) was greatly influenced by his experience of India and his contact with Hinduism. As we shall see, a change in attitude towards life manifests itself as a change in attitude towards art. What is important, then, is that Renoir should have found it necessary to write this book when he did, as a new ideological perspective was emergent in his work. That he should (perhaps unconsciously) have turned his back on modernist aesthetic theory and practice by looking to the example of his father is by no means irrelevant to what we can say about the site of meaning of the later films. So Renoir's new aesthetic is finally of a piece with a new philosophy. How this might be so is one of the things I want to examine in more detail.

The representation of the domain of art and artifice in the films of the fifties should not be thought of as a development peculiar to Renoir's work alone in these years. Its context is a world cinema that saw little innovation apart from experiments with flashy technology (3-D, widescreen) throughout a politically conservative decade retreating from the socially engaged film. It is remarkable just how many films of importance through the mid-fifties take art and artists as their subject: *Le Plaisir* (Max Ophuls, 1951); *Lola Montès* (Ophuls, 1955); *An American in Paris* (Vincent Minnelli, 1951); *Lust for Life* (Minnelli, 1956); *Limelight* (Charlie Chaplin, 1952); *Moulin Rouge* (John Huston, 1952); *The Golden Coach* (Renoir, 1953); *French Cancan* (Renoir, 1955). And there is another major group of French films for these years that have late nineteenth-century period settings: *La Ronde* (Ophuls, 1950); *Casque d'or* (Jacques Becker, 1952); *Les Belles de nuit* (René Clair, 1952); *Les Grandes Manoeuvres* (Clair, 1955); *Gervaise* (René Clement, 1956); *Elena et les hommes* (Renoir,

1956); *Une Vie* (Alexandre Astruc, 1958). Renoir, then, cannot be said to have arrived at the material for his films in isolation. Authors, positioned as subjects, are constituted in the ideological currents of their day. The larger historical context is so broad, however, that it would require a separate study to determine fully the impact of the post-world war II economic boom, the Cold War, and the competition from television (to mention some crucial forces) upon the ideological shape of this genre of fifties film production. Very early in the decade, writing about *The River*, André Bazin seems to have apprehended what was going on:

> Almost everything of any importance in the cinema of the past five years reveals in some way a spiritualistic inspiration, an optimistic humanism, a re-embracing of the ethical as opposed to social criticism or moral pessimism.[6]

Less charitably, of course, what Bazin is describing—if not defending—is the tasteful *cinéma de qualité* abhorred by the New Wave in general, attacked by François Truffaut in particular, and overturned by Jean-Luc Godard in practice.

What we can say about Renoir, then, without elaborating upon the circumstances he shared with so many other film makers of the decade, is that in contradistinction to the raison d'être for much of his work in the thirties, in the films of the fifties he is no longer interested in representing a social reality subject to the determinations of history. An unwillingness to admit this difference in Renoir's practice led some critics to chastise him for ignoring the appalling social conditions of India's cities or the Hindu–Moslem riots over Kashmir that exploded while he was filming *The River*, which it was felt he should responsibly have included in his treatment: "The misery and the overpopulation of India are not seen; they are simply the pretext for

---

[6] André Bazin, *Jean Renoir* (New York: Simon and Schuster, 1973), p. 116.

some beautiful plastic compositions, by which one would not have known a humane conscience to have been roused."[7]

While one may appreciate the critic's concern, his expectations are based on a misapprehension of *The River* compared with Renoir's earlier works. In *The River* man's social reality has no purchase in historical processes, rather, reality is but a transitory passage in an unending cycle of mutability. Unlike the films of the thirties, for example, the conception of justice in *The River* has nothing to do with the condition of man in society. When the innocent Bogey (Richard Foster) attempts to charm the cobra and dies from its bite, his death is to be accepted as the *natural* justice of an inevitable process of *natural* law to which one must learn to submit. To emphasise this lesson of submission to an essential mystery at the heart of all things, the film does not dwell on the moment of Bogey's death; instead, it lingers on his funeral, the plain wooden coffin heaped with colourful flowers and the stunned mourners in clumsy procession. The snake in Nature that claims Bogey is the film's symbol of that terrible justice which will lay claim to the evanescent lives of all of the characters.

But lives are not only evanescent in the sense that they will end, they are also caught up in the continuous passage of time, for which the film's great symbol is the flowing river itself. The basic conflict in the film is produced by man's struggle *against* accepting the necessity and inevitability of change. Hence the film centres on the passions of its characters, in particular on the turbulent feelings of the three adolescent girls, Harriet (Patricia Walters), Valerie (Adrienne Cori), and Melanie (Radha Sri Ram), and their infatuation with Captain John (Thomas Breen). Captain John, too, is troubled by passionate feelings, but his are not the fickle enthusiasms of adolescence, for he has come to Bengal to try and reconcile himself to the loss of a leg during

[7] Marcel Oms, "Renoir, revu et rectifié," *Premier Plan*, nos. 22-23-24 (May 1962), p. 46.

the war. More precisely, I should say that the film insists upon the *ephemerality*—although not the triviality—of all individual passion as the important theme, in view of the film's representation of this eternally mutable universe in which its characters struggle against death, disappointment, and disillusionment.

The ephemerality of individual passion seems to me a central thematic preoccupation of all of Renoir's films after 1950. This theme reaches conclusion with the last shot of "Le Roi d'Yvetot," the last episode of Renoir's last film, as the assembled characters dissolve the pain of adultery and the rancour of gossip in collective laughter. This insistence on the ephemerality of passion is certainly a departure from the work of the thirties. Many of those films contain murders enacted out of intense and absolute passion to produce a social justice that is collectively beneficial as well as personally satisfying. In the period of Renoir's political advocacy we would have to say that acts of passion were assumed to be instrumental to the transformation of society. By and large the films made after the war are without violence, however, so that their plots do not involve murder and betrayal, class consciousness or class action. The pressing conflict between social justice and institutional law crucial to the political intervention of those earlier films is gone. Renoir is no longer interested in party politics nor, evidently, in political solutions to human problems.

If *The River*, or *The Golden Coach* or *French Cancan*—or any of the films after 1950—are to be valued, they are not to be valued for the same reasons one values *La Chienne* or *Le Crime de M. Lange* or any of the films of the thirties. Not that my own response to each individual film or to the films of Renoir's two very different careers arises from a limitless critical flexibility. A knowledge of historical developments and ideological shifts necessitates adjusting one's expectations. Renoir's films do not now display the same confidence in the transformative possibilities of intense and absolute passion that they once did. Not fully understanding the change that has taken place in Renoir's work, some critics have suggested that this new, so-called philosophy of acceptance induces moral passivity when faced with situations calling for a responsible position. Renoir is not unaware that the world is fraught with great problems of possibly greater moment than ever before, and has spoken to his way of addressing them and to the change in his attitude:

> Before the war my way of participating in the universal concert was to try and raise a voice of protest. I do not think that my criticism was ever very bitter. I love humanity too much, so that I hope my sarcasm was always mixed with a little tenderness. Today, the new being that I am realises that this is not the time for sarcasm and that the only thing I can bring to this illogical, irresponsible, and cruel universe is my "love."[8]

Faced with a world of moral confusion, social corruption and political oppression is that what the bourgeois artist-intellectual is to do? Practically, Renoir may of course be wrong in the judgement he has made and the attitude he has adopted, but this is the direction he has taken and I think it is a mistake simply to conclude that it leads to moral passivity. In his own mind, Renoir has become quieter, but that is not the same thing as quiescent; he is less aggressive, less absolute, and recognizes that great passions can be totalitarian in their solution to great problems. "Love" (the quotation marks are Renoir's), like other commitments, can never be more than tentative in an "illogical, irresponsible, and cruel universe." I think there is something terribly sobering about this attitude, for all its apparent generosity, that it is even tinged by pessimism, for it now admits a much more provisional grasp of the world and of man in the world than ever before. We do not go on as if nothing had happened; we just go on because we must or will. To what

---

[8] Jean Renoir, "Quelque chose m'est arrivé," *Cahiers du Cinéma* 2, no. 8 (January 1952), p. 31

extent the provisional stance that lies behind this philosophy of acceptance informs *The River* remains to be seen.

There was an important aspect of experimentation to the production of *The River* in 1949-1950. While it was partially financed with American money, it was independently produced by Kenneth McEldowney far away from the time clocks and balance sheets of watchful studio executives. McEldowney, who knew India at first hand, admired Rumer Godden's novel, so he was prepared to let Renoir forgo the popular idea of an India of elephant dances, tiger hunts, and the like in favour of less commercial subject matter. The film makers chose to emphasise the confrontation of two cultures, Christian and Hindu, so Renoir and Rumer Godden set their narrative within the circle of an Anglo-Indian family. Renoir's addition to the characters in the novel of the figure of Melanie, a half-caste, serves to make the confrontation inevitable. But the confrontation is not social, as between the Italian Toni and the Parisian Albert; it is moral, religious, even philosophical. That there is no pretence at making a film about India other than as a Westerner might encounter it is clear from the outset. Behind the opening credits the customary welcome reserved for strangers to India is extended to the spectator of the film by the patterns we see drawn in flour on the floor of the house.

The River was Renoir's first film in colour and the first Technicolor film to be made in India. During the shooting, film had to be sent to the Technicolor labs in London for processing. Rushes were printed in black and white. Claude Renoir, who did the cinematography, had never worked with colour before either, and he and Jean evidently proceeded by trial and error. To the reliable if heightened artificiality of the Technicolor process Renoir manufactured sharper colour scales by having Eugène Lourié paint the grass occasionally, preferring to manipulate colour in front of the camera rather than relying solely upon lab effects. In all his future work with colour it became Renoir's usual practice to decorate the profilmic event to maximize the sense of artifice. The direct sound for *The River* was recorded on magnetic tape from Western Electric, the first time it had ever been used in motion pictures. Apart from Claude Renoir, Eugène Lourié, and the sound engineers, the remainder of the crew was Indian with limited experience.

The freedom of technique and subject and circumstance surrounding the making of *The River* allowed Renoir a freedom of narrative construction quite outside the conventions of American practice but of vital importance to the film's thematic interests. Unforeseen circumstances played their part. Shooting had been set to begin 20 November 1949, but was twice-delayed due to the late arrival of blimped cameras from London. Renoir took advantage of these postponements to shoot some documentary footage with an unblimped camera and no direct sound. The script which he and Rumer Godden had prepared from her novel was loose enough to permit the inclusion of documentary observations of Indian customs and Hindu ritual. Encouraged by his first trials, Renoir was inclined to divagate from the pursuit of a single dramatic story-line and to shoot many more documentary sequences than he had intended. Eventually, in the course of production, he shot enough footage to enable him to add to a more or less conventional dramatic fiction about Harriet's encounter with life within the circle of her Anglo-Indian family documentary material not strictly supported by either the dramatic action or the dialogue, but justified by an alternative conception of narrative construction. He also added the mature Harriet's voice-over commentary. The characters of the dramatic action are Anglo-Indians, Westerners effectively, or like Melanie pulled hither and thither between the conflicting demands of East and West. All of the documentary footage, on the other hand, without exception, depicts purely Indian life or religious ceremony. This documentary material consists of the festival of lights at Diwali, the shots of the statues of Kali, the return of her images to the river, the shots of life on the river, the sequence of the stairs, the story of Krishna and Radha, and the shots of the river and of spring at the film's conclusion. When editing the film at the Hal Roach studios in Hollywood, Renoir diminished the manifest story-line with each successive montage, gradually interpolating the documentary footage until he had a work that violated accepted narrative convention yet still seemed to please preview audiences: "The result was that the extraordinary ambience of place imposed itself on us little by little and became a new element in the story, probably the most important."[9] In this way the film becomes something of a meditation upon the conflicting ideals represented by Eastern and Western values and the differing attitudes towards human experience represented by Hindu and Christian philosophies. Harriet's intermittent commentary-in-recollection inclines us to share her mature judgements and encourages our contemplative detachment; while, at the same time, the admixture of documentary and fictional modes allows what is signified by the former to situate thematically what is signified by the latter. As Renoir has said: "Without India, the encounter of little Harriet with life would have been very different."[10] I would say that the selected documentary material insists upon the existence of a timeless cycle of creation and destruction, which emphasises the ephemerality of passion in the relationships among the characters of the dramatic fiction. The Christian or Western attitude towards life is represented as struggle, a continual becoming, whereas the Eastern or Hindu view sees life as a state of being, ever-renewed and never-ending. I do not think the film suggests that the twain will meet or can meet; however, the encounter serves to place our culturally determined life—the only life that can be *ours*—in a different perspective, a perspective that might make our certitudes about the meaning and purpose of human endeavour somewhat more provisional.

Structurally, this perspective is achieved by interpolating the

[9] Ibid., p. 32.
[10] Ibid.

documentary passages with the dramatic action at judicious moments. Strictly speaking, only one of these passages might be called extradiegetic. However, they are all in a different mode, generally signified by the choice of subject, long shots and long takes, and the voice-over. Both the subject matter and the style of these passages serve to inflect our judgement of the relationships between the characters evolving in the dramatic fiction. For example, the festival of Diwali, the festival of lights held on the darkest night of the year and presided over by Kali, the goddess of eternal destruction and creation, is intercut with Harriet's adolescent awakening, her fluttering infatuation for Captain John. We are thereby meant to grasp the ephemerality of this naive private passion in a universe charged with the eternal cycle of love and death. At the same time, Harriet's mature voice-over both explains the meaning of the festival to us and encourages our emotional detachment from the fiction by alluding to the "romantic dreams of a silly little girl." Raymond Durgnat has observed that Harriet's commentary eliminates suspense and produces an emotional levelling of the narrative. Perhaps this is why other critics have complained of the slightness of the story in *The River* while praising the documentary passages, as though the two were inevitably separable. But the story *is* slight, and I think it is intended to be slight: three young women fall in love with Captain John, who is bitter about the loss of his leg in the war; Bogey dies from the cobra's venom; Harriet attempts suicide out of guilt and frustration; Captain John counsels Harriet and finds that he can leave India with purpose in life renewed; a new baby is born. The importance of the story is its *relative* unimportance, even the lack of strong social definition among the characters and the indifferent acting performances serving to reduce any sense of great moment. We cannot be sure that the characters within the fiction see their situations quite like this, but the stance the film adopts insists upon our privileged awareness.

No sequence is more effective at privileging our awareness

over that of the characters than the masterful performance within the film of Harriet's retelling of the story of the Lord Krishna and the Lady Radha. To my mind, this is the centre of *The River*, both thematically and stylistically. In a present-tense voice-over Harriet narrates the birth and growth of the Lady Radha and the ceremony of her marriage to the Lord Krishna while we see the story performed by Melanie and Anil in the roles of the two principals. The presentation of this sequence is unlike any other in the film. Elsewhere Harriet's extradiegetic voice-over comments belong to the past tense of adult reflection, but here her narration is part of the diegesis, since it is addressed in present time to Captain John and Valerie, even if they are but half-attentive. However, the visual performance of the Krishna–Radha story is clearly extradiegetic since the spectator to the film is the only privileged observer. The notion that the Krishna–Radha story is intended to situate or comment upon the characters and their relationships is supported by intercutting shots from the principal diegesis of Captain John and Valerie along with shots of Harriet and Melanie. Furthermore, the Krishna–Radha story is *The River* in microcosm: "it's about anybody," Harriet says. It is a story of metamorphosis, of a village girl's transformation into the Lady Radha, of her loved one into the Lord Krishna, and of their transformation back into village bride and bridegroom. And it is a story without end, for it begins again with the birth of a little girl. So it is a story of metamorphosis through cycles of repetition translated with difference.

There are various motifs belonging to the religious and natural realms by which the cyclical pattern of the Krishna–Radha story becomes integral to the principal diegesis of the film. The film begins in mid-winter with Diwali, the festival in memory of the eternal war between good and evil, and it ends with spring and the new year Holī festival—shots of flowering trees and eye-dazzling blossoms intercut with shots of a fine red aphrodisiac powder being thrown over everyone and everything. These festivals are directly related to the cyclical life of Nature. They are intended to ward off malicious influence, revive the vital powers of Nature, and ensure harmony. The complete harmony between the natural and spiritual worlds supports the Hindu belief that all the universe is God and God is everywhere. But what of man's place? There is the suggestion of metamorphosis and renewal there, too. Of metamorphosis, in Harriet's perception of herself as the ugly duckling determined to be a swan and in Melanie's account of her transformation from grub into butterfly when she adopts the sari. Of renewal, in Harriet's statement after her attempted suicide that she "came back to life"; in Captain John's resolve to "begin again" ("With everything that happens to you, with everyone you meet, you either die a little bit or are born"); in the new baby girl, as in the Krishna-Radha story, come to replace the departed Bogey.

Is man's place at one, then, with the realms of Nature and spirit? Ideally, yes; practically, no. Man cannot achieve harmony with the whole world without accepting pain and joy, love and death, for he is a sentient and conscious creature in a partially sentient and wholly unconscious world. Like Harriet, we despair in the face of death and will not go on as if nothing had happened; suffer bitterness and self-pity like Captain John; sorrow for the transience of individual feelings with Valerie (" 'it' is going"); or cannot be certain of our identities like Melanie ("Why do we quarrel with things all the time?") Man's situation is defined by struggle and resistance. Melanie has the right advice (which her expatriate Irish father, played by Arthur Shields, comes closest to being able to live), advice possible from her because she is a half-caste, when she urges that we "consent, to everything." That is the wisdom of India which is to be learned from this encounter with an alien culture. Melanie's consent is surely another expression of the theme of endurance and faith that underlies *The Southerner*. It is advice apparently justified by Renoir's idealist conviction, indeed by the Hindu conviction, often repeated by Renoir in later life, that "the world is one."[11]

[11] In "On me demande ... ," for example, in *Cahiers du Cinéma* 2, no. 8 (January

But Melanie's advice is no more than provisional, for it is uttered by her without enthusiasm in the film, since man's condition, man's nature even, is to refuse consent, to struggle against accepting his relative insignificance and the mutability of his being in the world. Although the film would seem to conclude optimistically, with Captain John having achieved wisdom out of infirmity and the baby having come in the new spring, the last camera movement passes up over the heads of the three wistful girls looking into the distance to the river. The conflict between eternal change and human yearning remains to haunt us still: "The river runs, the world spins; the story ends, the end begins."

If Western man, in the ordinary practice of his life, will fall short of accepting his oneness with all creation, there is nevertheless a realm in which he may momentarily achieve a sense of fulfilment and catch a glimpse of that ideal harmony for which he longs. That realm is the realm of art. And here is where the extradiegetic privilege of the Krishna–Radha sequence is especially important. Why is it Harriet who tells the story of Krishna and Radha? It is worth remembering that in the film Harriet is a would-be poet, one of the many artist figures common to Renoir's films of the fifties; consequently, I believe her story invites us to consider the function of art in relation to this new philosophy of acceptance. In her own interests, there seems no doubt that Harriet tells her story out of a desire for a complete and harmonious vision of the world. Elsewhere in the film her model human relationship—perhaps an appropriate model for an adolescent girl—is the intense, absolute, and ultimately destructive passion of Antony and Cleopatra, a wholly Western story of struggle and finality. But Harriet's private interests as a character are not entirely what is at stake, given the conditions of representation of the Krishna–Radha story within the film. Since Harriet's voice-over is intermittent and secondary, since the sequence is not situated either historically or socially within

---

1952), p. 8, where Renoir writes of "this vast world which the Hindus say is 'one,' and of which, according to them, we are only a part, just like a tree, a bird, or a pebble."

the fictional world of the film and there is no audience diegetically present, it is *our* attention, *our* senses even, that are to be charmed by colour and music and dance. We are the implied audience for this spectacle. The treatment of this sequence, in its style, its formal completeness, and its narrative self-sufficiency within the text of the whole work is undoubtedly the most beautiful and satisfying in the entire film. Furthermore, the presence of this sequence does nothing to advance the plot of *The River*, so that it stands as a virtual set piece, an independent tableau. It does give an extraordinary aesthetic pleasure that "speaks out" to the spectator from the principal diegesis surrounding it because the conditions of its enunciation establish the primacy of the spectator–spectacle relationship. The value of the Krishna–Radha sequence in *The River* lies as much (or more) with what it *is* than what it is about. The making of a work of art is cause for celebration, for affirmation, even, at man's potential for achieving oneness with all creation. Art represents the satisfaction of human yearning in a world of eternal change because through its *formal* accomplishment man conceives the ideal condition of his being in the world. The immediate spectacle of the Krishna–Radha story entirely achieves our mediation with Nature (i.e., with our own natures) because it resolves the contradictions of lives in process through the momentary, imaginary unity of the subject for the enunciation with the object of its attention. In this sequence and this sequence alone is the theme of consent fully realized. If Renoir has now taken a more provisional view of human endeavour, then the function of art in this "illogical, irresponsible, and cruel universe" would seem to be consolatory. This, perhaps, is the fuller meaning of the "love" that the artist may bring to his fellows. Art may console us momentarily for the evanescence of our lives and feelings. When Harriet says that her story is about "anybody" she must mean that through it Melanie and Anil, Captain John and Valerie, Harriet and ourselves may cease our "quarrel" and find the fulfilment of desire. That the pleasure art may give is at the expense of our pain and disappointment we will learn further from *The Golden Coach* and *French Cancan*.

The Golden Coach and *French Cancan* clearly foreground the meaning and purpose that Renoir has discovered for art and the artist in this "illogical, irresponsible, and cruel universe." In the first place, both films are about artists and their art, Camilla and the commedia dell'arte in the former, Danglard and the Moulin Rouge in the latter. Camilla (Anna Magnani), who plays Columbine in the commedia, and her company of players arrive in the New World at the same time as a fabulous golden coach which has been ordered from Spain by the Viceroy (Duncan Lamont) of these regions as the symbol of his office. The players erect a stage in the courtyard of the local inn and perform without profit for the native population. It is not until the egoistic bullfighter, Ramon (Riccardo Rioli), attends a performance, applauds Camilla, and falls in love with her that popularity is assured. Ramon's rival is the gentle Felipe (Paul Campbell), Camilla's self-appointed business manager. When the troupe is eventually summoned to perform before the court, their financial success is assured. Camilla's directness pricks the stuffy formality of the courtiers but charms the Viceroy, who promptly falls in love with her. The Viceroy secretly attends Camilla's performances before the local population while openly sending her lavish gifts. Apparently dismayed by Camilla's frivolity and convinced of the hopelessness of his attentions, Felipe goes off to become a soldier in the colonial wars and leaves the field of love to Ramon and the Viceroy. The latter's most splendid gift of all to Camilla is the golden coach. However, the Viceroy's gift is premature, for his Cabinet of Ministers will only grant him the funds he needs to fight the war on condition that he withdraw his offer of the coach to "that common actress." If he persists in his folly, he is to be deposed. While he hesitates, Camilla runs to Ramon, who also insists that she return the coach, for she must have no other suitor than himself. At this point Felipe returns from the wars, avers that the Indians are much more civilised than we are, and urges Camilla to give up the golden coach so that she may start a new life with him close to Nature. Upon learning that the Viceroy is about to sacrifice his career for her, Camilla charitably donates the coach to the Church and returns to her métier, thereby cooling her rivals' jealousies and resolving all conflict in the film.

In *French Cancan* Danglard (Jean Gabin) is the impresario of "Le Paravent Chinois," a Paris club that specializes in variety acts and features La Belle Abbesse (Maria Félix), an exotic dancer and Danglard's current mistress. One evening, Danglard, La Belle Abbesse, and some fashionable customers go slumming in Montmartre where they visit "La Reine Blanche" and dance the popular *la chahut* with the working-class clientele. Danglard is attracted by Nini (Françoise Arnoul), a little laundress, despite the rebuffs of her jealous boyfriend, Paulo (Franco Pastorini). When Danglard next encounters Nini he has formed the idea of converting the energy of *la chahut* into a spectacular dance number to be called "le French cancan." For a sum, Danglard persuades Nini's mother to release her from the laundry and he sends her to Madame Guibole's dancing school along with the other neophytes chosen for the chorus line. A great deal of screen time is taken up showing the girls rehearsing and refining the new dance steps under Danglard's watchful eye. However, Danglard's attention to Nini arouses not only the jealousy of Paulo, but also the fury of La Belle Abbesse. At the dedication ceremony for the construction of the Moulin Rouge La Belle Abbesse sets upon Nini, and Paulo attacks Danglard, whereupon Baron Walter (Jean-Roger Caussimon), Danglard's financial backer and the Abbesse's "protector," withdraws his support for the project. Undismayed, Danglard continues his rehearsals while construction stands idle. Opportunity arrives in the form of the wealthy Prince Alexandre (Gianni Esposito), who takes over the backing of Danglard because he too is in love with Nini. When La Belle Abbesse opens the eyes of the naive and lovesick Alexandre to the fact that Nini is Danglard's mistress, he attempts suicide. A romantic interlude with Nini eventually consoles him for his loss, while his brush with death reconciles La Belle Abbesse to Danglard's artistic scheme. On opening night the crowd presses into the Moulin Rouge, but as the cancan is announced Nini refuses to go on stage because she is jealous of Danglard's latest protégé, Esther Georges (Anna Amendola). After a stern speech from Danglard about an artist's obligations to the public, Nini renounces the world for the theatre and leads the cancan dancers amidst the cheering spectators. Danglard is momentarily content with the roar of the crowd.

One's interest is unlikely to be compelled by the plots of these films, for they are so loose as to be inconsequential, and certainly not memorable. (The effort to find substance in the slightness of one and coherence in the confusions of the other taxes the memory quite enough.) Renoir has had a word or two to say on this matter:

> The subject of *French Cancan* is decidedly childish and about as surprising as that of a Western. I feel myself drawn more and more towards these kinds of stories, stories weak enough to leave me free to amuse myself with the cinematic.[12]

> The Romantics displaced the value of the work into the unfolding of events, into the surprise of an unexpected ending, into what we call 'suspense.' We still suffer from this heresy.[13]

Narratives that involve strong hermeneutic and proairetic codes, that is, a continually forward complicating movement arising from the intersection of character and action that demands resolution, such narratives sustain our interest by making choices available to the characters, choices allowed plausibility

---

[12] Jean Renoir, "*French Cancan*," in *Ecrits 1926-1971*, ed. Claude Gauteur (Paris: Belfond, 1974), p. 276.

[13] Jean Renoir, "*Le Carrosse d'or*," in *Ecrits 1926-1971*, p. 274.

because of the psychological and social bearings of the characters. The availability of choices and the making of choices is what propels the narrative. These choices allow for suspense, surprise, and sudden turns of events. This familiar narrative strategy implies a particular view of the world, of man and of history. It is one that is progressive—in the widest possible sense. That is why the full flowering of the novel in Western Europe belongs to the great period of industrial and colonial expansion of the nineteenth century. Novels—at least the traditional classical novels—are about makers and seekers, the histories of individuals (or nations) plunging forward into time (and frequently extending themselves in space). But there are other kinds of narrative with other implications, narratives in which intrigue, suspense, and surprise do not figure to any great extent—at least not to the extent that our attention is compelled by these devices—and in which choice is not the available, overwhelming psychological, moral, or social option placed before the characters. Such narratives are not so much progressive as static—again, in the widest possible sense—and we have to look elsewhere than to the protagonist's forward movement through space and time, and other than to his or her power (or powerlessness) before events for an understanding of man and his world. Such narratives presuppose a different view of man and of history. Perhaps they create a view of the world that man is asked to accept, in which he is asked to come to terms with what is. If *The Golden Coach* and *French Cancan* are narratives of this latter type, that is because of our disregard for their feeble plot/intrigue in favour of our acceptance of their commanding presence as we watch them, of their insistent *formal* existence for us.

In advancing the tendency towards artifice begun with *The River*, *The Golden Coach* and *French Cancan*, along with *Elena et les hommes* (1956), are marked by a degree of stylisation in every respect that situates them firmly within a cinema of spectacle. With these films Renoir has completely relinquished external realism—"Je n'ai pas tourné mon film au Pérou"—and any pretence at psychology of character—"Je ne veux pas faire de psychologie"[14]: "Today I am going through a period of my life where I try to distance myself from external realism and find a more composed style, closer to that which we call 'classical.' "[15] This distance is achieved first of all by eschewing contemporary subjects in favour of displacement into an historical past: the eighteenth-century colonial Peru of *The Golden Coach*, the late 1880s in France for *French Cancan* and *Elena et les hommes*. These milieux have the equivalent function of the strangeness of India seen through Western eyes in the documentary passages of *The River*: they create a distance from contemporary social realities. Nor is there an attempt at an historically accurate period re-creation—in the manner of *La Marseillaise*, say—in any of these late films, for unlike that earlier film they do not have the political or social function of making the past resonant for our own time. The controversial General Boulanger is obscured by the somewhat foolish character of General Rollan in *Elena et les hommes*, and even the historical identity of Ziegler, the founder of the Moulin Rouge, has been disguised as Danglard. Colonial Peru is a fiction concocted on the sound stages of Cinecittà, while the gay Paris of the eighties is self-evidently a confection of the French studios. Environment has utterly lost the specificity and history the determining force we might have been accustomed to expect from a film credited to Jean Renoir. Renoir once remarked that the Paris of *Monsieur Verdoux* is not the historical Paris; it is a world created by Chaplin not intended to bear any resemblance to reality.[16] Like Chaplin's Paris or Ophuls's turn-of-the-century Vienna, Renoir's milieux in the colour films of the fifties are worlds of his own fabrication.

[14] "Je n'ai pas tourné mon film au Pérou" is the title of an article written in 1953 and reprinted in *Ecrits 1926-1971*, pp. 272-273. Renoir wrote "Je ne veux pas faire de psychologie" in 1955, and it too is reprinted in *Ecrits 1926-1971*, pp. 277-280.

[15] Jean Renoir, "*Toni* et le classicisme," *Cahiers du Cinéma* 10, no. 60 (June 1956), p. 2.

[16] Renoir, "Je n'ai pas tourné mon film au Pérou," p. 273.

The Golden Coach apart, in his later life Renoir returned over and over again to the twenty-five years prior to the First World War for the settings for his prose writings as well as his films. The novel *Le Crime de l'anglais* (1979) is set in the Bourgogne in 1883, while the biography *Renoir, My Father* (1962) is an account of a segment of French artistic and social life in the latter half of the nineteenth century through to the First World War. In 1953 Renoir was working on a screenplay for a film on the life of Van Gogh which would concentrate on his early years leading up to the meeting with Gauguin in 1888. Of special fascination for Renoir seems to have been the period known as *la belle époque*, the decade immediately before the war, for it is evoked by Jeanne Moreau's song "Quand l'amour meurt" in *Le Petit théâtre de Jean Renoir* and is the period setting for the greater part of the two novels *Les Cahiers du Capitaine Georges* (1966) and *Le Coeur à l'aise* (1978), as well as for the abortive film project *Julienne et son amour* (written in 1968, published in 1979):[17]

> For this film I started to be interested in the period—the period before the war of 1914. I dreamed of laces, beautiful interiors, paintings by Bonnard and Vuillard, etc. That was one of the things that, in the beginning, attracted my attention.[18]

[17] Interestingly, "le coeur à l'aise" is a line from "En revenant de la revue," the most famous of the popular songs written to celebrate General Boulanger's national acclaim after his famous review of the troops at Longchamps on Bastille Day 1886. In *La Règle du jeu* the fête at La Colinière is entitled "En revenant de la revue," and there the performance of the song is part of the bitter satire of the house guests for their conservative attitudes and right-wing views. Boulangism, after all, with its cult of the hero and its militarism, was a species of fascism. That Boulanger is the basis for Rollan in *Elena et les hommes* is transparently evident. That the lying, philandering, opportunistic general should be so trivialized is distressing.

[18] From an interview with Alexander Sesonske, "Renoir: A Progress Report," *Cinema* 6, no. 1 (1970), p. 18. Of "Quand l'amour meurt" Renoir wrote, in *My Life and My Films*, that "Jeanne Moreau takes us for a little while outside our century of sleazy progress" (p. 277).

This attraction notwithstanding, it is difficult to say precisely why Renoir became enchanted with the late nineteenth century and *la belle époque*, although, as I have suggested, it is possible to take note of the consequences. Perhaps the very unreality of *la belle époque*, "the good old days" later generations of Frenchmen were fond of recalling for their stability and promise before the crush of war, perhaps this unreality contributed to the fascination. It must have seemed a golden age, the stuff of myth and legend, and yet a perilous Eden whose attractions were edged in the memory by the knowledge that it clung to the other side of the watershed of that Great War which accelerated the enormous social, economic, and political developments of our century:

> The event which most greatly influenced the Frenchmen of my generation was the First World War. It is doubtful whether western civilization will survive its present madness, but if our species does not wholly disappear, and if historians still exist a few centuries hence, they will be able to divide the chronicle of our time into two stages—before and after 1914.[19]

One should remember that *la belle époque* was the period of Renoir's youth, the period of his father's universal fame, whose reminiscences the young Renoir recorded in 1915 to let lie until the 1950s when he began writing *Renoir, My Father*. In his later works Renoir makes no effort to extinguish the glow surrounding *la belle époque*. From about 1951 on he seems purposely to illuminate his youth and obscure his political maturity in the thirties. As he weaves through his "spell of memories" in *My Life and My Films* (1974) from his present-day situation in America, he regards France and the past with undisguised nostalgia. He confesses to being a man of the nineteenth century who

---

[19] Renoir, *My Life and My Films*, p. 40.

185

identifies his personality with his familial roots, who finds there the precepts that have formed his character and his films.

One important consequence of Renoir's enchantment with the later nineteenth century in his work since 1950 has been to essentialize the historical past. In distancing the films from contemporary social realities through displacement, and in deliberately artificializing the period re-creation so that historical referents lose their specificity, the past becomes fixed, unaltering and unalterable, caught in a representation that places it outside any articulation of history as process. Renoir bears no historical witness; the films appear to witness nothing so much as their own existence as works of art. In contradistinction to the effectivity of the film work during the thirties, these "histoires fausses" permit Renoir to abjure historical modes of determining value. The basis for making judgements, for making an active intervention in the course of human affairs, loses its contingency, so that what is valued becomes essentialized, not to say eternalized and universalized. Thus what was seen to be valued once becomes of fixed value now, transcending any recognition of process or contradiction. The past uses the present, instead of the present using the past. We can then begin to understand why Renoir's theorization of his position—if that is the proper phrase—in his late prose works is resolutely antimodernist, in favour of an idealist aesthetic he associates with his father. It will also become apparent why this aesthetic is consistent with a consolatory rather than an interrogative function for art.

The films of the fifties further ensure their distance from external realism and topicality by spectacularizing their settings and foregrounding their studio artifices. One should not ignore, one should instead notice the factitious backdrops that serve for la Butte de Montmartre in *French Cancan*, and the studio floor that passes for the bullfight arena or the camera setups from the "fourth wall" that reveal the proscenium arch as the space of performance in *The Golden Coach*. In these films the revelation of the mise-en-scène becomes a signifier of performance.

Whereas in India Renoir had on occasion to paint the grass green to assert the sharp colour scales he wanted, studio work permitted him to denature his settings utterly and exercise an absolute technical control over every aspect of production. In the later films there is deliberate cultivation of artifice in the decor, the costumes, the styles of performance of the actors, and sometimes in the delivery of lines of dialogue. Where the acting seems clumsy and unschooled, for example, I would suggest that Renoir wants a tangible gap between the actor and the role so that the performer will *not* get under the skin of his or her part. Thereby any semblance of verisimilitude, any possibility of three-dimensionality or individuality in the characters is destroyed. Renoir has admitted that his great concern in working with Anna Magnani on *The Golden Coach* was to guard against her persona carrying her in the direction of the conventions of psychological realism: "many people were astonished that an actress famous for her portrayal of stormy emotion should have been used in a piece more suited to a Milanese puppet-show."[20] And of Ingrid Bergman in *Elena et les hommes* Renoir has said that she "contrived with her usual genius to portray a character as unrealistic as the settings."[21] The characters in these late films are to be accepted as nothing more nor less than stock types in the tradition of popular romance or boulevard theatre: the type of the bullfighter, the Viceroy, the apache, the Prince. And they are to be recognized as such by the broadly gestural, even melodramatic styles of performance that reduce them to virtually one dimension. Paulo's adolescent rage and Prince Alexandre's theatrical self-pity at Danglard's seduction of Nini in *French Cancan* are clarifying examples. The air of the "Milanese puppet-show" dominates every gesture, squashes every nuance, and turns moments of high drama into farce. In these artificialized settings characters are never *in* an environment; they move in

[20] Ibid., p. 267.
[21] Ibid., p. 266.

front of it. So we cannot accept that such typological beings as they are have grown out of it, have been determined by it. Their costumes, too, are not designed to help them incarnate social naturalism.[22] Gone, then, is the socialization of space that distinguishes a film like *Toni*, in which what the characters say and feel and do is a function of their social condition. *The Golden Coach* and *French Cancan* are films in which our discussion, or our interest, can never be guided by their superficial concern for character and motive and social identity.

In a review of *The Golden Coach* Tony Richardson remarked that it was the unnatural vibrancy in the use of colour which set these later films apart in the manifestation of their artifice:

> Its beauty lies, unusually, in colour rather than the compositional values. Renoir uses simple light settings, the interiors of pale, natural woods, the exteriors of mellowed plaster, and the costumes are in subdued violets, lemons and blues. Against these are set the bright scarlets, the sharp cobalts of the players. In every shot there is some note off key—the decoration on a chair, the jewel on a cravat—

[22] In *French Cancan* the dress of the characters, like the settings, frequently alludes to art, not life. Most critics have observed the extraordinary echoes of the Impressionists, of Degas (the dancers, of course), Manet (the hard-edged, primary colour contrasts), Pissarro, Renoir, and even of Delacroix, Corot, and Van Gogh. For example, the costumes, the setting, and the dance at "La Reine Blanche" obviously recall Renoir's *La Moulin de la Galette*, which was painted in Montmartre. But it is André Bazin, in his *Jean Renoir*, who places the appropriate emphasis upon the inspirational function of these echoes here, as opposed to what would be their merely decorative value in other hands: "The camera does not film a re-created painting for us (as in *Moulin Rouge*); it operates easily and naturally from inside the painter's conception" (p. 135). For Bazin, Renoir's camera captures the spirit of the paintings, beyond their existence as material objects for copying. I think, too, that the innumerable allusions are a reminder of just how much of this film is worked up from an artistic reality, that it is the representation of the idea of a representation, in many respects a self-contained visual world without any reference to a social reality. When we see a character or a scene dressed or arranged in a manner that gives us a felt apprehension of the world of painting, perhaps of the work of a particular Impressionist painter, our willing belief in the convention of the naturalistic unity of characterization is inevitably suspended and our attention to the forward progress of the narrative is diverted.

that gives the whole harmony an added strength and vibrancy.[23]

One must not conclude from this lavish and proper description that colour is pejoratively understood as mere decoration, that it is some distraction from our centre of interest. Rather, the profusion of colour is inherent to the meaning and purpose of the film. André Brazin describes our first sight of Esther Georges, going about her business as a chambermaid, before Danglard transforms her into a street singer:

The woman bustles about in the half shadow of the room, then turning around, leans out of the window to shake out her dustcloth. The cloth is bright yellow. It flutters an instant and disappears. Clearly this shot, which is essentially pictorial, was conceived and composed around the brief appearance of this splash of yellow. It is equally clear that the event is of neither dramatic nor anecdotal significance. The flash of yellow remains purely pictorial, like Corot's spot of red, but in eclipse.[24]

Bazin offers this as an example of the way in which pure pictorialism in film can induce in the spectator a subjective moment of contemplation in the midst of the flow of events. Every critic and every spectator seems to have his or her privileged moment of colour delirium. My own, apart from the whirling kaleidoscope of the cancan, comes when Danglard is walking after Nini on a Montmartre street. He stops before the bright yellow door of a closed carriageway and a street peddler holds up towards him a white and green cauliflower. Dramatically irrelevant, the shot lasts but a few seconds, and yet draws attention to itself in its stunning juxtaposition of colours. To the centrality of colour as a means of foregrounding the artifice of *The Golden Coach*

[23] Tony Richardson, "*The Golden Coach,*" *Sight and Sound* 23, no. 4 (Spring 1954), p. 199.
[24] Bazin, *Jean Renoir*, p. 132.

and *French Cancan* I would add the companion importance of music and dance. *The Golden Coach*, for example, makes Vivaldi *visible*. This music is no mere accompaniment to the narrative or the ephemeral passions of the characters; it has an extradi-egetic life of its own, so that it competes for our equal attention with the colour and the mise-en-scène. Similarly, in *French Cancan*, when the Prince escorts Nini around the Paris cafés, the music and the songs of the Café-Conc' have little or nothing to do with the ostensible plot but offer their own independent delight. Edith Piaf and Patachou deserve the billing they are awarded in the film's credits. And then, triumphantly, one's appetite for music, colour, and movement is fully satisfied by the astounding conclusion to *French Cancan*.

I believe that this new formalism in the late films, this com-mitment to a non-naturalistic style in Renoir's work after 1950, is consistent with his frequent devaluation of the importance of the subject, akin to the painter eliminating his figurative motif, consistent, in other words, with his new-found interest in the work of his father, the other Impressionists, and the post-Impres-sionists ("Bonnard, Vuillard, etc."):

> Towards 1870, a group of young men whom we have since dubbed the Impressionists believed they could liberate art of all traces of literature. After fifty years of effort, they had brought their public to the point of accepting that in a painting, or in a piece of music, the subject was secondary. I remember my father's great anger concerning one of those paintings representing a young girl delicately inclining her head which a dealer thought he could commercialize by calling it *La Pensée*. Furious, Renoir exclaimed: 'In my paintings one doesn't think!'[25]

> Among seekers of truth, painters perhaps come closest to discovering the secret of the balance of forces in the uni-

[25] Renoir, "*French Cancan*," p. 276.

verse, and hence of man's fulfilment. That is why they are so important in modern life. I mean real painters: the great ones. They spring up in little groups in periods of high civilization. Scientists, like painters, also strive to probe this secret. The authentic, the really great, pierce through the outward appearance of things. The problem is a very simple one, that of giving back to man his earthly paradise.[26]

Renoir alleges that through his mastery of form alone can the artist penetrate the world of appearances to reveal the essential truths of human experience. What, then, is the social function of art? How does art "give back to man his earthly paradise?" This "problem," as Renoir puts it, may be "a very simple one," but the solution is not so easily agreed upon. Renoir himself has represented quite contrary solutions in the course of his career. In the thirties Renoir conceived his artistic practice as an interrogation of the forms of society, as an intervention in the processes of history. Now, in the fifties, as we have seen, history seems to have stopped, to have become essentialized, and instead of an advocacy of a specific partisan politics, there is an advocacy of art as the only restorer of man's earthly paradise. If political solutions will not ameliorate human problems, perhaps aesthetic solutions will.

The centrality of colour, music, and dance at the expense of a consequential plot or consequential characterizations places the late films in the category of the *divertissement*. That does not mean that we are to treat these films lightly; the category helps to grasp their function. Renoir has subtitled *The Golden Coach* "une comédie fantaisiste" while *French Cancan* is "une comédie musicale." So both belong to a genre in which we expect to see problems resolved in harmony. Both are comedies and both are about the theatre, or at least specific forms of popular entertainment. In so far as *The Golden Coach* celebrates the commedia dell'arte, it regards it as an entirely folk art, so that it is pointedly

---

[26] Renoir, *Renoir, My Father*, p. 448.

shown to be despised by the pretentious court party in the film. And the cancan of *French Cancan* is shown to have evolved directly from the popular, working-class *la chahut*. It is not until Danglard visits a Montmartre dance hall, "La Reine Blanche," and is enticed to join in *la chahut* with the low life of Paris, that he gets the inspiration for the cancan. Later, his Moulin Rouge will be built on the very site of his inspiration, the old "La Reine Blanche." Camilla and Danglard are entertainers, not politically conscious artists, and their arts are unpretentious, produced without the soul-searching or the exhibitionism of the Romantic imagination which Renoir has so come to loathe. Their self-announced artifice, their stylisation, their theatrical locus, and the very notion of the *divertissement*, make it clear that *The Golden Coach* and *French Cancan* are "about" performance and the space of performance. (And within the space of performance I mean to include the spectator.) It is, as I have said, the consistent spectacularization of the mise-en-scène that is the signifier of performance in these films. That does not mean, as some critics have suggested, that the films offer an ironic commentary on the uncertainties of identity, on role-playing à la Pirandello, or that they moralize about that obsessive critical shibboleth, the confusion of illusion with reality, theatre with life.[27] What it does mean is that we see how, why, and with what consequences art and artifice are being created.

These entertainments foreground the art of their artists: Camilla (*The Golden Coach*), Danglard (*French Cancan*), Miarka (*Elena et les hommes*), Cordelier/Opale (*Le Testament du Docteur Cordelier*), Gaspard (*Le Déjeuner sur l'herbe*), Ballochet (*Le Caporal épinglé*), Georges (*Orvet*), and Renoir himself (*Le Petit théâtre de Jean Renoir*). *The Golden Coach* opens with a long shot

---

[27] I make this point despite Camilla's often quoted line: "Where does the theatre end and life begin?" It does not seem to me that the remark is offered as a generalizable profundity about the confusion of illusion and reality so much as a felt expression of her own particular confusion at that moment in the fiction, caught up as she is with the attentions of three suitors whom she must renounce for her art.

of the closed curtain on a proscenium stage. Then the camera tracks forward and the curtain rises to reveal the court stage set. Gradually, as the world of the film opens up, we move outside the court to other spaces (some of which are also stages, or give the impression of being stages: the playing spaces of the commedia dell'arte at the inn and at court; the internally framed spaces in the palace; the corrida; four conjoined rooms at court which, in a long scene, are always represented from the "fourth wall," so that the camera slavishly, and obviously, respects the 180-degree line). When Camilla finally takes possession of her prized golden coach about two-thirds of the way through the film, she turns to the astonished court party and admonishes them that it is customary to bow to the *comédienne* at the end of the second act! At the film's conclusion we return to the court stage set with which the film opened, the camera tracks back, the curtain falls, and Camilla and Don Antonio (the master of ceremonies) are left alone in front of the proscenium. We should be reminded that *we* are the audience seated in the orchestra attending to the events of the film taking place on a stage (or a stage within a stage) commanded by Camilla and her troupe of players. We have seen Camilla as Columbine in the commedia dell'arte, and we have seen Camilla's artful resolution of all differences within the world of the fiction which contains the commedia. The twenty or so minutes given over to the performance of the show at the conclusion of *French Cancan* indicate that the entire drive of that narrative is finally towards Danglard's orchestration of this eye-catching, breathtaking spectacle— performed both for *our* benefit as spectators and as the happy resolution of Danglard's affairs. Renoir is the director of *Le Petit théâtre de Jean Renoir*, and he appears beside a toy stage draped in red velvet to introduce the film and the first episode, and then reappears to introduce each of the three remaining episodes in turn. Renoir's role as both the *metteur-en-scène of* the fiction and *within* the fiction encourages us to regard the amazing succession of artist figures in the previous films as surrogates for himself or, at the very least, as stand-ins for an *idea* of the artist. At one remove from the films themselves, then, what is signified is Renoir's own art, his amusement with "the cinematic," his fascination with performance and the space of performance.

The artist figures in Renoir's late films all bring their "love" (even the perversity of Cordelier/Opale tests the rule) to an "illogical, irresponsible, and cruel universe." Within the fictions of *The Golden Coach* and *French Cancan* the "love" of Camilla and Danglard consists of their talent for reconciling the world's differences through their arts, even at some cost to themselves. The worlds of these two films are worlds of petty jealousies (Paulo, La Belle Abbesse, the Viceroy) and of fragile ambitions (Felipe, Ramon, Baron Walter). Such disorderly and nagging human feelings are not only destructive of social harmony, they are also too ephemeral to justify the absolutism with which people act on them. Camilla settles the intrigues of the court and cools the passions of her lovers with her gift to the Church of that symbol of worldly vanities, the golden coach ("Where gold commands, laughter vanishes"). All social distinctions are abolished as the entire cast of the film/fiction assembles on the court stage to hear the Archbishop make a speech of reconciliation on Camilla's behalf in which he invites the entire court retinue, the inhabitants of the city, and the company of players to hear Camilla sing at high mass. All of the actors applaud, and Camilla turns downstage through the proscenium in front of the final curtain. If this is a world in which everyone is appeased, it is also a world in which no one is punished. Here, and in *French Cancan*, there is to be no moral accounting for human foible or misdemeanour. As with the conclusion of *Le Petit théâtre de Jean Renoir*, where again the cast of the film/fiction turns and bows to the audience, forgiveness is all. When Danglard, the consummate impresario, introduces his crowning act, the formal, aesthetic accomplishment of the dance is cause for collective celebration, is shown to be the condition for everyone's *consent*. The cutaways to close-ups of the major characters during the performance of the cancan show that all are reconciled in and through the dance—the characters with one another, ourselves with the characters. Inspired by the conviviality of the occasion, couples link arms in two-shot after two-shot; Baron Walter proposes to marry La Belle Abbesse; and Paulo's rage at Danglard and his yearning for Nini gradually subside until we see him last with his arm around Nini's friend. The cancan itself is not performed on the stage at the Moulin Rouge, but in the midst of the audience and surrounded by the audience. Finally, everybody is caught up in the dance; "la famille du Moulin Rouge" (Danglard's words) is one with the entire world. The performance of the cancan within the achievement of the entire film is an instance of how art satisfies human yearning through an image of ideal harmony. Here and now is the ideal condition of one's being in the world, the momentary restoration of man's earthly paradise. It is the function of art to console for our little wretchedness and compensate for our fallible human natures. Like the Krishna–Radha sequence in *The River*, *The Golden Coach* and *French Cancan* gratify our wish for a complete and harmonious vision of the world. This happens within the films, in the resolution brought about by each, which testifies to the triumph of art and the artist, and between the films and ourselves in the pleasure each gives. The universe within the films and outside the films is now seen to be a little less illogical, irresponsible, and cruel.

I have said that Camilla and Danglard each produce a *coup de théâtre* that resolves the conflicts in these films at some cost to themselves.[28] Both Camilla and Danglard must renounce personal relationships for a social relationship with an audience. "Why am I a success on the stage," asks Camilla, "while in life I destroy everything I love?" At the conclusion of *The Golden*

---

[28] This expressive phrase, *coup de théâtre*, is Tom Milne's, in his essay on Renoir's films after 1939 in *Cinema: A Critical Dictionary*, ed. Richard Roud (London: Secker & Warburg, 1980), p. 850.

Coach, as Camilla stands before the final curtain, having re-
nounced the world's vanities, Don Antonio asserts that she belongs to the theatre but asks whether she misses her three lovers.
"A little," Camilla replies. For Danglard, personal relationships
are temporary affairs, never absolute passions, and that is the
drift of his admonition to Nini before her dressing-room door
when she delays the start of the cancan by trying to make her
claim on him a condition of her performance. Jealous of Danglard's new discovery, Esther Georges, Nini has to be told that
the artist's métier means serving the public at the sacrifice of
one's self. And while the cancan is being performed to the delight
of the crowd, Danglard sits backstage, alone, keeping time to
the music. Danglard's age, Camilla's sorrow, their common isolation, is, I believe, the reservation to the entire world's harmony
proposed by these films. Like the last camera movement in *The
River*, here, in the fates of Danglard and Camilla, is an acknowledgement of human yearning still, a reminder of the provisional nature of the consent that is being urged upon us. It is
this lingering tension between art and Nature (our natures) that
makes the consolatory function of art provisional.

Despite this tension between art and Nature, a view of art
that would console us for our condition certainly does not aim
to transform it. I said of the presentation of the Krishna–Radha
sequence in *The River* that it resolves the contradictions of lives
in process through the imaginary unity of the spectator with the
spectacle. The world, as Renoir would wish it, is become one.
But if our consolation is at the expense of any acknowledgement
of life's contradictions, then the spectator-as-subject becomes
fixed in illusionist immediacy outside any possibility of articulating change. This is a representation to be consumed, not acted
upon. Our individual and collective desire for social harmony
is not to be fulfilled in social practice but in aesthetic experience.
This is consistent with the strong witness that these late films
bear to their own self-contained existence as works of art, sac-
rificing any specificity towards contemporary social realities, and

essentializing the historical past. The knowledge produced by this aesthetic is of a fixed and unalterable world. This view and practice of art is fundamentally idealist, and the subject for this practice is a transcendental subject. Consequently, the subject positioned in this way is also trapped in a position of *ideological* fixity. "Illusionists have a social value," says Danglard to one of his performers. Indeed, and that value has social consequences. For if it is the function of ideology to make social relations intelligible, then the idealist aesthetic of the late films would justify an attitude towards social matters that is extremely conservative:

> I don't believe that responsibility in an author ever worked. I don't believe that any author ever did any good because he was feeling a responsibility. I believe some authors instinctively feel a certain love for the human being, and they will do a lot of good, I hope. And some of the ones don't, and that's all.[29]

This explains Renoir's promotion of the popular or folk arts, like the commedia and the cancan (or the cinema), and his support for a Camilla and a Danglard (or Miarka and Gaspard et al.), and the elevation of a certain perception of his father.

The idea of the artist that emerges from Renoir's late works is of one who lacks political consciousness and is driven by intuition rather than intellect and prefers instinct over reason. The art of such an artist is not made according to abstract principles or to satisfy a theory: "A swallow speeds through the air to catch a gnat and to satisfy its hunger; not to verify a principle."[30] Despite all assertions to the contrary, an aesthetic solution to human problems is still, however, a political solution. It was Pierre-Auguste Renoir's theory that one should let oneself be carried like a cork in life's stream, the so-called philosophy

---

[29] James Silke, "Jean Renoir on Love, Hollywood, Authors, and Critics!" *Cinema* 2, no. 1 (February 1964), p. 14.

[30] Renoir, *Renoir, My Father*, p. 67.

of acceptance adopted by Jean Renoir, which justified the elder Renoir's proud claim that "in painting there are no poor."[31] That, one might say, is actually the *cost*, in social terms, of an idealist aesthetic. In *Renoir, My Father* Jean quotes with approval his father's comment upon his experience during a painting tour of Southern Italy: "All the Calabrians I met were generous, and so cheerful in the midst of their poverty. They made you wonder if it's worthwhile to spend your time earning money."[32] The reader may be able to acquiesce in Pierre-Auguste's nineteenth-century certainties, but the younger Renoir would also adopt them as his own. Elsewhere he writes:

> Renoir did not see the world like other men. In his view nothing was absolutely black or white. That explains how he could live through the Commune and other important events witout taking sides. He was aware that labels and classifications existed, but a label did not guarantee the contents of the bottle.[33]

That may be an explanation of the moral and political perspicacity of Renoir *père*, although it does not follow that any such self-justification would have occurred to him. For Renoir *fils*, on the other hand, a fine disclaimer may be appropriate after the disillusionment of his involvement in the politicized thirties. One should contrast Renoir's present distrust of absolutism with Octave's earlier terror at the moral irresponsibility of a society in which everyone has his own relativistic "good reasons." What is Renoir's art now but our wish-fulfilling desire?

[31] Ibid., p. 381.
[32] Ibid., p. 236.
[33] Ibid., p. 146. Compare these remarks with Renoir's comments in *My Life and My Films* (p. 124) about the "meaningless" separation of mankind into fascists and communists.

BOOKS AND ARTICLES BY JEAN RENOIR

"La Bête humaine." *L'Avant-garde*, no. 780 (6 October 1938). Reprinted in *Image et Son*, no. 315 (March 1977), pp. 26-27.

La Chienne. *L'Avant-Scène du Cinéma*, no. 162 (October 1975).

"Cinéma." *Cahiers de la Jeunesse*, no. 17 (15 December 1938), p. 24. Reprinted in *Image et Son*, no. 315 (March 1977), p. 28.

Ecrits 1926-1971. Edited by Claude Gauteur. Paris: Belfond, 1974.

"The First Version of *The Crime of M. Lange*." In *Jean Renoir*, by André Bazin. New York: Simon and Schuster, 1973.

La Grande Illusion. Paris: Balland, 1974.

[Introduction]. In *Renoir (1841-1919)*. Los Angeles: Dalzell Hatfield Galleries, 1943.

"The Issue: Questions and Answers on Peace and War." In *Film: Book 2*. Edited by Robert Hughes. New York: Grove Press, 1962.

"Jean Renoir Discusses His Past, Present, and Future." *The Cine-Technician* 4, no. 20 (March-April 1939), pp. 177-179, 206.

Lettres d'Amérique. Edited by Dido Renoir and Alexander Sesonske. Paris: Presses de la Renaissance, 1984.

My Life and My Films. New York: Atheneum, 1974.

"On me demande. ..." *Cahiers du Cinéma* 2, no. 8 (January 1952), pp. 5-8.

"Quelque chose m'est arrivé." *Cahiers du Cinéma* 2, no. 8 (January 1952), pp. 31-32.

La Règle du jeu. *L'Avant-Scène du Cinéma*, no. 52 (October 1965).

Renoir, My Father. Boston: Little, Brown, 1962.

Rules of the Game. Translated by John McGrath and Maureen Teitelbaum. New York: Simon and Schuster, 1970.

"Souvenirs." *Le Point*, no. 18 (December 1938), pp. 275-286.

Reprinted in *Jean Renoir* by André Bazin. New York: Simon and Schuster, 1973.
This Land is Mine. In *Twenty Best Film Plays*. Edited by John Gassner and Dudley Nichols. New York: Crown, 1943.
"*Toni* et le classicisme." *Cahiers du Cinéma* 10, no. 60 (June 1956), pp. 1-3.

BOOKS ABOUT RENOIR

Bazin, André. *Jean Renoir*. New York: Simon and Schuster, 1973.
Beylie, Claude. *Jean Renoir: le spectacle, la vie*. Paris: Editions Seghers, 1975.
Braudy, Leo. *Jean Renoir: The World of His Films*. Garden City, N.Y.: Doubleday, 1972.
Cauliez, Armand-Jean. *Jean Renoir*. Paris: Editions Universitaires, 1962.
Durgnat, Raymond. *Jean Renoir*. Berkeley and Los Angeles: University of California Press, 1974.
Faulkner, Christopher. *Jean Renoir: A Guide to References and Resources*. Boston: G. K. Hall, 1979.
Gauteur, Claude. *Jean Renoir: La Double Méprise (1925-1939)*. Paris: Les Editeurs Français Réunis, 1980.
Gilcher, William. "Jean Renoir in America: A Critical Analysis of His Major Films from *Swamp Water* to *The River*." Ph.D. diss., The University of Iowa, 1979.
Leprohon, Pierre. *Jean Renoir*. New York: Crown, 1971.
Mast, Gerald. *Filmguide to "The Rules of the Game."* Bloomington: Indiana University Press, 1972.
Poulle, François. *Renoir 1938 ou Jean Renoir pour rien?* Paris: Editions Cerf, 1969.
Premier Plan, nos. 22-23-24 (May 1962). Edited by Bernard Chardère.
Serceau, Daniel. *Jean Renoir, l'Insurgé*. Paris: Le Sycomore, 1981.

Sesonske, Alexander. *Jean Renoir: The French Films, 1924-1939.* Cambridge: Harvard University Press, 1980.

ARTICLES AND INTERVIEWS ABOUT RENOIR

Agate, James. "Funny and Not So Funny." In *Around Cinemas.* London: Home and Von Thal, 1946.

Agee, James. *"The Southerner."* In *Agee on Film.* New York: McDowell, Obolensky, 1958.

Bonitzer, Pascal, Jean-Louis Comolli, Serge Daney, Jean Narboni, and Jean-Pierre Oudart. *"La Vie est à nous,* film militant," *Cahiers du Cinéma,* no. 218 (March 1970), pp. 44-51.

Brunelin, André-G. "Jacques Becker, ou la trace de l'homme." *Cinéma 60,* no. 48 (July 1960), pp. 87-111.

Bussot, Marguerite. "Propos de Jean Renoir." *Pour Vous* (25 January 1939). Reprinted in *Jean Renoir* by André Bazin. New York: Simon and Schuster, 1973.

Fauchois, René. "Réconciliation autour de *Boudu." Cinéma 56,* no. 7 (November 1955), pp. 71-72.

Gauteur, Claude. *"Boudu sauvé des eaux* de Fauchois à Renoir." *Image et Son,* no. 184 (May 1965), pp. 49-56.

Harcourt, Peter. "A Flight from Passion: Images of Uncertainty in the Work of Jean Renoir." In *Six European Directors.* Harmondsworth: Penguin Books, 1974.

Hennebelle, Guy. "Jean Renoir (1894-1979) and the Militant Cinema." *Cineaste* 9, no. 4 (Fall 1979), p. 61.

"Il y a 35 ans *La Marseillaise."* Edited by Claude Gauteur. *Image et Son,* no. 268 (February 1973), pp. 1-78.

Jeanson, Henri. *"La Marseillaise* ou les fourberies de Stalin." *La Flèche de Paris* (19 February 1938). Reprinted in *Image et Son,* no. 268 (February 1973), pp. 66-70.

Leenhardt, Roger. "Le Cinéma: *Le Crime de M. Lange." Esprit,* 4, no. 42 (1 March 1936), pp. 975-977.

Leenhardt, Roger. "Jean Renoir et la tradition française," *Intermède*, no. 1 (Spring 1946), pp. 102-110.

Marie, Michel. "The Poacher's Aged Mother: On Speech in *La Chienne* by Jean Renoir." *Yale French Studies*, no. 60 (1980), pp. 219-232.

Nichols, Dudley. "The Writer and the Film." In *Twenty Best Film Plays*, edited by John Gassner and Dudley Nichols, pp. xxxi-xl. New York: Crown, 1943.

Nogueira, Rui, and François Truchaud. "Interview with Jean Renoir." *Sight and Sound* 37, no. 2 (Spring 1968), pp. 56-60.

"*La Règle du jeu* et la critique en 1939." Edited by Claude Gauteur. *Image et Son*, no. 282 (March 1974), pp. 49-73.

Richardson, Tony. "*The Golden Coach*." *Sight and Sound* 23, no. 4 (Spring 1954), pp. 198-199.

Rivette, Jacques, and François Truffaut. "Renoir in America," *Sight and Sound* 24, no. 3 (July-September 1954), pp. 12-17.

Roud, Richard, and Tom Milne. "Jean Renoir." In *Cinema: A Critical Dictionary*, edited by Richard Roud, pp. 835-854. London: Secker & Warburg, 1980.

Sarris, Andrew. "Boudu Saved from Drowning." *Cahiers du Cinema in English*, no. 9 (March 1967), p. 53.

Serceau, Daniel. "1934: Un film précurseur, *Toni*, de Jean Renoir." *CinémAction*, no. 8 (Summer 1979), pp. 67-69.

Sesonske, Alexander. "Renoir: A Progress Report." *Cinema* 6, no. 1 (1970), pp. 17-20.

Silke, James. "Jean Renoir on Love, Hollywood, Authors, and Critics!" *Cinema* 2, no. 1 (February 1964), pp. 12-15.

Strebel, Elizabeth Grottle. "Renoir and the Popular Front." *Sight and Sound* 49, no. 1 (Winter 1979/80), pp. 36-41.

Truffaut, François. "Comme il y a vingt ans: *La Grande Illusion* de Jean Renoir est d'une brûlante actualité." *Arts*, no. 691 (14 October 1958), p. 7.

RELATED BOOKS AND ARTICLES

Althusser, Louis. *Lenin and Philosophy and Other Essays*. London: NLB, 1971.

Barthes, Roland. *Mythologies*. London: Paladin, 1972.

———. *S/Z*. New York: Hill & Wang, 1974.

Brogan, Denis. *The Development of Modern France (1870-1939)*. London: Hamish Hamilton, 1940.

Buchsbaum, Jonathan S. "Left Political Filmmaking in France in the 1930s." Ph.D. diss., New York University, 1983.

Carné, Marcel. "Quand le cinéma descendra dans la rue?" *Cinémonde*, no. 85 (1930).

Caute, David. *Communism and the French Intellectuals (1914-1960)*. New York: Macmillan, 1964.

Chardère, Bernard. "Jacques Prévert et le Groupe Octobre." *Premier Plan*, no. 14 (November 1960), pp. 71-91.

Comolli, Jean-Louis, and Jean Narboni. "Cinema/Ideology/Criticism." In *Movies and Methods*, edited by Bill Nichols, pp. 22-30. Berkeley and Los Angeles: University of California Press, 1976.

Coward, Rosalind, and John Ellis. *Language and Materialism*. London: Routledge & Kegan Paul, 1977.

Eagleton, Terry. *Marxism and Literary Criticism*. London: Methuen, 1976.

Editors of *Cahiers du Cinéma*. "John Ford's *Young Mr. Lincoln*." In *Movies and Methods*, edited by Bill Nichols, pp. 493-529. Berkeley and Los Angeles: University of California Press, 1976.

Fofi, Goffredo. "The Cinema of the Popular Front in France (1934-1938)." *Screen* 13, no. 4 (Winter 1972/73), pp. 5-57.

Foucault, Michel. "What Is An Author?" *Screen* 20, no. 1 (Spring 1979), pp. 13-29.

Lefranc, Georges. *Histoire du Front Populaire (1934-1938)*. Paris: Payot, 1965.

Marcus, J. T. *French Socialism in the Crisis Years 1933-1936*. New York: Praeger, 1958.

Oury, Pascal. "De Ciné-liberté à *La Marseillaise*." *Le Mouvement Social*, no. 91 (April-June 1975), pp. 153-175.

Rebérioux, Madeleine. "Théâtre d'agitation: Le Groupe 'Octobre.'" *Le Mouvement Social*, no. 91 (April-June 1975), pp. 109-119.

Rhode, Eric. *A History of the Cinema*. Harmondsworth: Penguin Books, 1978.

Rohdie, Sam. "Totems and Movies." In *Movies and Methods*, edited by Bill Nichols, pp. 469-480. Berkeley and Los Angeles: University of California Press, 1976.

Sarris, Andrew. "Notes on the Auteur Theory in 1962." In *The Primal Screen*. New York: Simon and Schuster, 1973.

———. "Towards a Theory of Film History." in *The American Cinema*. New York: E. P. Dutton, 1968.

Strebel, Elizabeth Grottle. "French Social Cinema and the Popular Front." *Journal of Contemporary History* 12, no. 3 (July 1977), pp. 499-519.

———. "French Social Cinema of the Nineteen Thirties: A Cinematographic Expression of Popular Front Consciousness." Ph.D. diss. Princeton University, 1974.

Talon, Gérard. "Le Cinéma du Front Populaire." *Cinéma 75*, no. 194 (January 1975), pp. 34-56.

Williams, Raymond. "A Lecture on Realism." *Screen* 18, no. 1 (Spring 1977), pp. 61-74.

Wood, Robin. "Ideology, Genre, Auteur." *Film Comment* 13, no. 1 (1977), pp. 46-51.

205

CHRISTOPHER FAULKNER
is Associate Professor of Film Studies at
Carleton University in Ottawa. He is the author
of *Jean Renoir: A Guide to References and
Resources* (G. K. Hall).

LIBRARY OF CONGRESS CATALOGING-IN-PUBLICATION DATA

FAULKNER, CHRISTOPHER.
THE SOCIAL CINEMA OF JEAN RENOIR.

BIBLIOGRAPHY: P.
INCLUDES INDEX.
I. RENOIR, JEAN, 1894- . I. TITLE.
PN1998.A3R428 1986   791.43'0233'0924   85-43276
ISBN 0-691-06673-6